Cambridge Elements ≡

Elements in Applied Linguistics
edited by
Li Wei
University College London
Zhu Hua
University College London

KONGISH

Translanguaging and the Commodification of an Urban Dialect

Tong King Lee
University of Hong Kong

CAMBRIDGE
UNIVERSITY PRESS

Shaftesbury Road, Cambridge CB2 8EA, United Kingdom

One Liberty Plaza, 20th Floor, New York, NY 10006, USA

477 Williamstown Road, Port Melbourne, VIC 3207, Australia

314–321, 3rd Floor, Plot 3, Splendor Forum, Jasola District Centre,
New Delhi – 110025, India

103 Penang Road, #05–06/07, Visioncrest Commercial, Singapore 238467

Cambridge University Press is part of Cambridge University Press & Assessment,
a department of the University of Cambridge.

We share the University's mission to contribute to society through the pursuit of
education, learning and research at the highest international levels of excellence.

www.cambridge.org
Information on this title: www.cambridge.org/9781009281133

DOI: 10.1017/9781009281126

First published 2023

A catalogue record for this publication is available from the British Library.

ISBN 978-1-009-28113-3 Paperback
ISSN 2633-5069 (online)
ISSN 2633-5050 (print)

Kongish

Translanguaging and the Commodification of an Urban Dialect

Elements in Applied Linguistics

DOI: 10.1017/9781009281126
First published online: November 2022

Tong King Lee
University of Hong Kong

Author for correspondence: Tong King Lee, leetk@hku.hk

Abstract: This Element introduces Kongish as a translingual and multimodal urban dialect emerging in Hong Kong in recent years and still in the making. Through the lens of translanguaging and linguistic commodification, and using the popular Facebook page Kongish Daily as a case in point, the study outlines the semiotic profile of Kongish. It examines how Kongish communications draw on a full range of performative resources, thriving on social media affordances and a creative-critical ethos. The study then turns to look at how Kongish is commoditized in a marketing context in the form of playful epithets emplaced on locally designed products, demonstrating how the urban dialect is not merely a niche medium of communication on social media but has become integral to commercial, profit-driven practices. The Element concludes by challenging the proposition that Kongish must be considered a 'variety' of English, arguing instead that it is an innominate term embodying translanguaging-in-action.

Keywords: Hong Kong, Kongish, translanguaging, commodification, urban dialects

ISBNs: 9781009281133 (PB), 9781009281126 (OC)
ISSNs: 2633-5069 (online), 2633-5050 (print)

Contents

1 Kongish: A Multimodal Translingual Practice

In postcolonial languaging, dispossession is the key that opens unexpected doors.
Behind those doors lie the vast, wondrous troves of xenophonic énoncés.
— Rey Chow, *Not Like a Native Speaker*

1.1 Introducing Kongish

This study investigates an emergent and still evolving semiotic phenomenon peculiar to the sociolinguistic environment of Hong Kong: Kongish. A simple gloss on the term 'Kongish' may derive formulations along the lines of 'Hong Kong-style English' or 'English codemixed with Cantonese Chinese elements'. Citing an editorial in Hong Kong's *South China Morning Post* (*SCMP*) of 11 June 1987, Bolton (2002a: 3), for instance, notes the increasing use of English in the local community, such that 'Hongkong [*sic*] English has evolved into an incipient patois, an inevitable process in any colonial setting where the imported tongue cannot avoid absorbing the characteristics of the vernacular, especially one as vibrant as Cantonese'.

Descriptions such as the above are formulated in relation to Hong Kong English (HKE). They are, however, inadequate, indeed slightly misleading, in relation to Kongish, the focus of the present study. Hence, my point of departure is that English as it is used in Hong Kong has often been identified alongside other members of World Englishes (Kirkpatrick 2021), Asian Englishes (Bolton et al. 2020), or Postcolonial Englishes (Schneider 2009). This is exemplified in the *SCMP* quote above, which speaks of the incipient formation of HKE as 'an inevitable process in *any* colonial setting' (emphasis added). It is also evidenced by the creation of a Hong Kong component within the International Corpus of English (ICE-HK) (Nelson 2006; Wong 2017: 6–9). Underlying such a conception is Kachru's (1985, 1992 [1982]) concentric hierarchy of Englishes, in which Hong Kong belongs by definition to the so-called Outer Circle, alongside other former British or American colonies (Singapore, India, Philippines, and so forth), where English is instituted as an official language as a result of historical contingencies. In this model, what has come to be called HKE would belong to a peripheral variety of English, as implied by the visuality of the concentric circle model.[1]

---

[1] Although, as Bolton (2002b: 30) has argued, the objective of Kachru's model is to 'kill off such "sacred cows of English" as the "native speaker" versus "non-native" speaker dichotomy', and to instead view the use and acquisition of English from a pluricentric perspective; the inside-to-outside design of Kachru's concentric circles arguably gives rise to the suggestion of a centre-periphery order. And despite Kachru's best intentions, the notion of native versus non-native speakership has continued to operate in the Outer Circle (and certainly in the Expanding Circle) till this day, including among users of English in Hong Kong; see Hansen Edwards (2015: 197).

This study espouses the view that Kongish, currently still in the midst of its making, should be considered beyond the rubric of English and, as a corollary, be distinguished from HKE. It is a native urban dialect based around English but at the same time distinguishes itself from English in form, on a conscious and metalinguistic level on the part of its practitioners. More radically, Kongish may perhaps be said to exceed language as such, morphing itself into a translingual but also multimodal register by tapping into the material-technological affordances of social media and text-based artefacts.

This is not to say that Kongish, as I describe it here, does not share characteristics with World, Asian, or Postcolonial Englishes, and in particular with HKE. On the contrary, it is probably fair to say that Kongish bears a genealogical relation to HKE. According to a definition by researchers from the Education University of Hong Kong, HKE refers to

> the English spoken by native Hong Kongers with its *special accent and characteristics*. It is primarily spoken by those whose first language is Cantonese and it is often considered as the *Hong Kong variant of China English*. According to Kachru's model, the line between Outer Circle [and] Expanding Circle is not always clear in Hong Kong. Like *an institutionalized 'Outer Circle' variety*, English in Hong Kong has a legal status as an official language and the written form is widely used in various contexts, such as governmental documents and public notices.[2]

On this definition, we can see how HKE as a variety of English is positioned equivocally as lying somewhere between the Outer and Expanding Circles in the Kachruvian model. This corroborates Cummings and Wolf's (2011: x) observation that '[t]he exact status of HKE may still be a matter of debate among linguists and the informed public', even though the fact that it is uniquely shaped by its colonial history and socio-political environment is beyond dispute. What is crucial for us in these and many other similar descriptions is that they represent a prevailing view of HKE, namely that it is an *offshoot* of English, albeit one exhibiting distinctive characteristics. The researchers at the Education University of Hong Kong, on their part, were specifically interested in phonetic issues, developing a spoken corpus of HKE 'to help teachers, learners and researchers have a better understanding of *the major problems in learning English pronunciation* by Hong Kong, Mainland Chinese and non-Chinese *speakers in Hong Kong*'.[3]

Lest it be misunderstood, I hasten to emphasize that, pedagogically speaking, the above project is a meaningful and perfectly respectable one. The point I am

---

[2] https://corpus.eduhk.hk/english_pronunciation/index.php/background-of-china-english-and-hong-kong-english/ (emphasis added).

[3] https://corpus.eduhk.hk/english_pronunciation/ (emphasis added).

making here is that HKE has hitherto been conceived as some kind of *problem*, a contentious entity whose identity begs precise definition. This belies the assumption that it is an aberration, even if a creative and unique one, from 'standard' or British English – the perennial point of reference for English as it is used in Hong Kong. Therefore, the linguistic profile of HKE, whether in terms of phonetics, lexicogrammar, or discourse, is premised on its difference with 'standard' English (for an overview of the relevant literature, see Wong 2017: Ch. 1). In recent years, however, a vernacular register based around English, but departing radically from English in general and HKE in particular, has emerged in Hong Kong's semiotic landscape, both on social media and in the commercial market. It is properly speaking an urban dialect, which we shall (for want of a better term) refer to as Kongish.

1.2 Kongish versus HKE

The immediate question to be raised concerns the ontological identity of Kongish, that is, whether and how it is related to and differentiated from English in general and HKE in particular. On this point scholars differ in their views. Some do not make a distinction between Kongish and HKE; for example, when Hansen Edwards (2016: 158) holds that '[t]here is also evidence that HKE is gaining greater acceptance in Hong Kong, as illustrated by the establishment of Kongish [Daily]', she implicitly conflates HKE and Kongish, treating them as synonyms. In her study on the lexicogrammar and discourse of HKE, Wong (2017: 163) makes a single mention of Kongish at the very end of her conclusion, maintaining that it represents how 'present-day HKE can be viewed as being a newly emerging, nativised variety of English', hence implicitly understanding Kongish as a more contemporary manifestation of HKE and a localized variation on English. Others, for instance, Sewell and Chan (2016), recognize Kongish as 'a new label' (p. 597) existing alongside the longer-standing term HKE. While observing similarities and differences between the two, both authors remain ambivalent as to 'whether Kongish is seen as a variety (or not), as the real Hong Kong English (or not), or as a passing fad (or not)' (p. 606).

Yet other scholars contemplate Kongish as altogether transcending the World/Asian/Postcolonial Englishes paradigm. Li Wei, in particular, argues that in virtue of its dynamism and spontaneity, Kongish defies such categorical labels as 'Chinese', 'Hong Kong Chinese', 'English', 'Hong Kong English', 'China English', or 'New Chinglish' (Li et al. 2020: 315–16). Accordingly, he does not consider creative communications in Kongish (and for that matter, in Singlish, or colloquial Singapore English, as well) as innovations *in English* or any *single, named language*. They challenge the very notion of language by transcending the boundaries of named languages and the boundaries between language in the narrow sense of conventionalised speech and writing and other semiotic means, including colour, scriptal system, size, space, image, and sign. (Li 2020: 246; emphasis added)

Clearly, Kongish as it is described by Li Wei is quite a different creature from HKE as expounded by other linguists. First and foremost, Kongish is a distinctively written medium. This contrasts with HKE, which is more often studied as a spoken phenomenon, although there is extant research on English as it is written in Hong Kong, in both pedagogical and commercial contexts.[4] One might say that Kongish taps into the speech resources of HKE and *re-semiotizes* them into a written medium (whether exchanged on social media or entextualized on text-based artefacts), hence transcending the divide between text and talk. More than that, Kongish is multimodally generated through interactions between linguistic text and what are traditionally called para-, extra-, or non-linguistic modalities – 'colour, scriptal system, size, space, image, and sign'. It is an inherently intersemiotic medium.

It would perhaps be apt at this point to provide some illustrations to exemplify the formal differences between HKE and Kongish. For HKE, a most convenient resource is *A Dictionary of Hong Kong English* (Cummings & Wolf 2011), subtitled *Words from the Fragrant Harbor*, where 'fragrant harbor' is a calque of the Chinese word for Hong Kong. A few examples would suffice to show that HKE comprises (a) English words that have come to take on different meanings than in British or American English; (b) locale-specific acronyms or abbreviations; and (c) words transliterated from Cantonese (and to a lesser extent, Mandarin[5]).

Belonging in the first category is the word *banana*, which in HKE does not denote the fruit, but is rather an idiomatic derogatory term referencing ethnic Chinese persons with Western cultural dispositions, be it in terms of their accent or mannerisms. The logic of this analogy is that a banana has a yellow skin and white flesh, and this inside-outside difference in colour metaphorically extends to ethnic Chinese persons (who have 'yellow' skin, as stereotypically described) who nevertheless culturally identify themselves with Western, or 'white', people (Cummings & Wolf 2011: 11). The acronym FILTH, specific to Hong Kong's colonial history, illustrates the second category. It stands for 'Failed In London Try Hong Kong', referring to British persons who seek to develop their careers in London but eventually move to Hong Kong after failing

---

[4] For an annotated bibliography of HKE research, see Setter et al. (2010: 117–29).

[5] Mandarin refers to the standard form of spoken Chinese based on the Beijing dialect. In Hong Kong, it is more often denoted by the term Putonghua – literally, common language.

in their endeavours in the UK (Cummings & Wolf 2011: 57). Finally, an example of a word from the third category is *dai pai dong*, which transliterates the Cantonese word denoting the once-ubiquitous street food stalls catered to the working class (Cummings & Wolf 2011: 46). It is worth noting, however, that *dai pai dong*, along with several other words associated with HKE, have been included in the *Oxford English Dictionary* (*OED*) since 2016.[6] This 'consecration', so to speak, of HKE in the *OED* already problematizes the boundary of named languages or language varieties, an issue to which we shall return later.

In a more extended example below, provided by Wong (2017) on the basis of the ICE-HKE corpus, <indig> marks the indigenous word *dim sum*, referring to a type of Cantonese cuisine comprising small pieces of food items contained in round bamboo baskets. The final utterance by Z exemplifies a classic case of codemixing, where a Cantonese word is inserted into an otherwise relatively well-formed English utterance, and where the onset and termination of the 'mixing' in question are clearly delineated:

A: Yes but uh what we meant by family day uh nowadays is not something that we should follow

A: It's not is not so straight. But uhm maybe it is what our practice

Z: Uhm uhm uhm uhm

A: What we usually do

Z: So you would go to some <indig> dim sum <indig> uh place and . . . uh place and . . .

(Wong 2017: 119)

Compare this with Kongish, which draws on the broad lexical repertoire of HKE, among other resources. Yet it also exceeds HKE by fusing it with other semiotic elements to generate a creative register that may be described as *translational*, in the sense that it embeds translation (especially calque and transliteration) into its discursive constitution. To cite a preliminary example, Figure 1 is an introduction to Kongish Daily[7], a Facebook page centred around Kongish that we will explore in more detail in the next section.

I will leave the passage in Figure 1 untranslated to demonstrate its markedness as a 'variety of English' – a designation we will retain for convenience at the moment, but with which I will take issue in the concluding section.

---

[6] https://public.oed.com/updates/march-2016-update-new-hong-kong-english-words/. Other HKE words included in the *OED* are: *char siu, compensated dating, kaifong, guanxi, lucky money, sandwich class, milk tea, shroff, sitting-out area, siu mei, yum cha*, and *wet market*.

[7] https://www.facebook.com/KongishDaily/.

Kongish Daily is a local site sharing news in Kongish.

Kongish ng hai exac7ly Chinglish.

The site is founded bcoz we want to collect relly research how people say Kongish by looking at everyone ge replies, including you and me, and share this finding to all people who think Chinglish = Kongish. But actcholly, Kongish =/= Chinglish; Kongish also =/= romanised Cantonese only; Kongish dou ng exactly hai Hong Kong English. If you ask little editers Kongish hai mud? Little editer can light light dick tell you: Kongish is a collective creation used and understood by Hongkongers ♥ <3

Only knowing English or Cantonese ng wui give you the full picture, you have to be a Hongkonger sin can fully understand our page, Kongish Daily 😑 :))

PS for secondary school chicken:
If you want to learn English, Sor(9)ly, this site ng wui help you learn more English, but to share news with you in Kongish, finish.

Figure 1 Kongish Daily's self-introduction.
Source: www.facebook.com/KongishDaily.

This introductory passage is metalinguistic – it is written in Kongish about Kongish – and encapsulates most of the urban dialect's salient features, explained in detail in Section 3. Briefly, these include: (a) a corrupted English morphology inflected with numerals (*exac7ly* [exactly], *sor(9)ly* [sorry]); (b) eye-dialect spelling (*relly* [really], *actcholly* [actually]); (c) symbols (=/=, meaning 'not equal to'; (d) emoticons (the yellow smiley face; the red-coloured heart shape followed by <3, where <3 is used among young Hong Kong girls in text messaging to express love/kiss); (e) abbreviations, or what David Crystal (2010: 190) calls 'textisms' (*bcoz* for 'because'; PS for 'postscript', though without the full stops that mark each letter); (f) calqued colloquial expressions from Cantonese (*secondary school chicken*, from *zung¹ hok⁶ gai¹* 中學雞); and (g) apparently English utterances undergirded by Cantonese syntax as well as calques and transliterations from Cantonese ('Kongish *dou ng* exactly *hai* Hong Kong English', where the main verb phrase *dou ng hai* is transliterated from the Cantonese phrase 'is not exactly'; 'Only knowing English or Cantonese *ng wui* give you the full picture', where *ng wui* transliterates 'will not' and the positioning of 'only' in the sentence-initial position comes from Cantonese grammar).

This example demonstrates a self-reflexivity that is characteristic of Kongish, designed to be consciously translingual and bicultural: it dresses itself as English, but ruptures the latter's flow and texture by continually inscribing the sounds and rhythms of Cantonese beneath the linguistic skin of the English language. It is worth noting that in the quote in Figure 1 from Kongish Daily, there is no typographical distinction between English and non-English segments by means of, for instance, italicization, bolding, or capitalization. Nor are tone numbers indicated for transliterations from Cantonese, which is the convention for romanized transcriptions (using, for instance, the *Jyutping* 粵拼 system) of Cantonese words in Hong Kong. All of this has the effect of rendering the non-English terms, mostly originating in Cantonese, as unmarked items when they are in fact highly marked from a standard English perspective. Hence, while English is presumably the matrix language (per Myers-Scotton 1997), the discourse at its most hybrid would appear sensible only from the perspective of a bilingual Cantonese-English user.[8]

Therefore, unlike HKE, there is an uncanniness to Kongish's identity as a putative variety of English, rendering it as enigmatic as it is confounding to the uninformed reader. A principal argument of this study is that Kongish communications cannot be adequately described in the traditional terms of codeswitching and codemixing, which, following the Myers-Scotton (1997) paradigm, refer to the activation of different language codes in alternation with

---

[8] The netizens engaged with Kongish Daily are generally Cantonese-English bilinguals in virtue of their education. Under Hong Kong's education system, English is a compulsory subject in government schools, which means by Form 4 (Grade 10 equivalent), an average Hong Kong student would have completed 10 years of English-language learning in school. Despite its status as an official language, English may or may not be frequently used among the local Chinese outside classroom time, for Hong Kong is a predominantly Cantonese-based society. Adding to the language matrix is Mandarin, or Putonghua, which has been incorporated into the school curriculum since 1998, which means the younger generation of local Hong Kong citizens would have a degree of proficiency in understanding and using Mandarin (including its standard romanization form, the Hanyu Pinyin), though Cantonese still remains the preferred language. Hence, in terms of their linguistic profile, the younger generation of local Chinese may be considered to possess a plurilingual repertoire.

each other – *one code at a time*. Rather, Kongish should be seen as a heterogeneous *repertoire* in metamorphosis – as opposed to a unitary code with discernible lexicogrammatical or discourse patterns – in which evolving resources from linguistic and extralinguistic modalities are orchestrated in tandem in complex and dynamic ways.

But it is not enough to recognize that Kongish and HKE are formally distinct based on the previous examples. One must push further and ask how the one relates to the other in light of Hong Kong's colonial history as well as its sociopolitical circumstances in the postcolonial era and in the broader context of global capitalism and high modernity – or, better still, liquid modernity (Bauman 2000). More specifically, if we accept that the English language represents the legacy of the British administration of Hong Kong spanning one-and-a-half centuries (1842–1997), and Cantonese, the (subjugated) mother tongue (at least during the colonial period) among the predominant ethnic Chinese population, the question that arises is this: what is the theoretical implication of the linguistic alchemy between English and Cantonese, embodied in a weaker sense in HKE and much more transgressively in Kongish, for understanding Hong Kong's language economy?

1.3 Languaging to Translanguaging

A possible angle on this question is to conceive of Hong Kong's language usage through the idea of *languaging*, a term attributed to A. L. Becker (1995). Languaging refers to the dynamic, processual, and historically embedded nature of language-in-action, as opposed to Language (with a capital L) as a static, closed, and stable system, or, in Ortega y Gasset's (1957: 242) words, 'as an accomplished fact, as a thing made and finished'. This conception, of course, invokes the Saussurean notion of *langue* versus *parole* – except that the theoretical premium is now on the latter, not the former.

Languaging spotlights the vicissitudes and nuances of mediated as well as situated interactions beyond the structural coordinates of language. It pertains to lived experiences that entail, but are not limited to, a narrow conception of linguistic communication. A classic definition is provided by Nigel Love (2017: 115), for whom languaging is

> a cover term for activities involving language: speaking, hearing (listening), writing, reading, 'signing' and interpreting sign language. As recommended by [Roy] Harris (1981, p.36), it remedies the lack of a 'specific superordinate verb which subsumes the common verbs to speak, to read, to write and to understand'. As a general term it is preferable to 'using language' or 'language use' in *not implying that what is used exists in advance of its use* [emphasis added].

For Love (see also Thibault 2011; Steffensen 2015; Cowley 2021), languaging describes the messy, 'first-order' state of language-in-action preceding language-as-structure (or Language), which belongs to a 'second-order' of things that derive from linguistic praxis. In other words, language as a system comes after the fact and as a result of languaging as praxis. This conception reverses the entrenched Saussurean notion of language as a pre-existing and static system of rules to be applied by users in real-time communication.

Hence, languaging highlights the flux and flow of semiotic actions as well as interactions comprising language as it is empirically used on the ground, with little regard to the rules, patterns, or boundaries characteristic of language as it is institutionalized in language policies, lexicographies, pedagogies, and so forth. Whereas language points to the clinical instrumentality of communication on the basis of a codified system of signs, languaging involves a to-and-fro articulation of identities and worldviews as well as a continual negotiation of memories, beliefs, and experiences against the contingencies of the here-and-now. On this understanding, language as a practice is more than communicating meaning; it is as much 'a process of using language to gain knowledge, to make sense, to articulate one's thought and to communicate *about* using language' (Li 2011: 1224; emphasis added).

With this in mind, I want to take a short detour via the notion of postcolonial languaging, developed by the Hong Kong-born and internationally renowned cultural theorist Rey Chow in her book *Not Like a Native Speaker* (Chow 2014). This recourse to Chow's work enables us to incorporate a cultural studies lens on languaging in postcolonial Hong Kong, which will go some way to helping us understand the socio-political milieu against which Kongish has emerged. Without this broader context in view, one might slip into a facile understanding of Kongish as a linguistic fad on social media, thereby missing the point about its language ideological thrust.

In an eponymous chapter in her book, subtitled 'The postcolonial scene of languaging and the proximity of the xenophone', Rey Chow begins with an episode during her graduate days, where her professor wrote a seemingly innocuous comment on her term paper: 'You have one of those things offered by a colonial education – a clear writing style' (Chow 2014: 35). On the face of it, the professor's comment was a compliment, but to Chow it gave rise to a feeling of uneasiness, for she felt stigmatized as the embodiment of an attribute (clarity of writing) that was purportedly the result of her being a colonial subject. With this incident in mind, Chow contemplates the relation between language and colonialism in respect of Hong Kong, specifically the 'protracted confrontation between languages, between the enforcement of the colonizer's language as the official channel of communication and the demotion of the colonized's languages as obsolete or simply irrelevant' (Chow 2014: 35).

Chow's strategy in rethinking this asymmetric confrontation from the perspective of the colonized is to theorize multilingualism from below (see Pennycook & Otsuji 2015: 9–13). In particular, she highlights languaging – which, as discussed above, precedes language – as a fundamental enunciative condition in postcolonial Hong Kong. A focus on languaging, or language in generative action, is meant to resuscitate that which is lost through the institutionalization of language under the colonial education system. More precisely, what language elides, and languaging captures, are 'such illegible and often unconscious elements . . . as accent, tone, texture, habit, and historicality as well as what is partially remembered, what is erroneous but frequently reiterated, and, ultimately, what remains unsaid and unsayable' (Chow 2014: 65).

Thus, whereas language as an apparatus of governmentality emanates from the establishment, languaging speaks to the dispossessed, whose enunciation is often subject to marginalization and erasure. Turning to Benjamin's notion of 'aura' (the touch of authenticity around a work of art) and Foucault's idea of *énoncé* (language as it is found, as already-said as opposed to originally formulated), Chow (2014) understands the enunciative field in Hong Kong as inherently multilayered and heteroglossic. In this enunciative field, situated exchanges between English and the local vernacular accrue over time into 'an archiving in process, involving shifting series of transitions among different levels of deposits, remains, excavations, and adaptations' (p. 57). Languaging is the archiving of enunciative idiosyncrasies in the here and now.

What crystallizes from these exchanges is not an aberration of or inferior derivation from a primary or original model of communication based around British English and Received Pronunciation. Rather, it is an 'emergent languaging domain' that 'draws its sustenance from mimicry and adaptation and bears in its accents the murmur, the passage, of diverse found speeches' (Chow 2014: 59). These accents, tones, and textures, including 'what is partially remembered, what is erroneous' (Chow 2014: 65), constitute the 'aura' (à la Walter Benjamin), so to speak, of the processual languaging of the dispossessed people, that tinge of authenticity afforded the utterance of the locale, which, far from a reproduction of the colonizer's language, revels in its own carnivalesque heteroglossia.

Calling this domain of postcolonial languaging the Xenophone, Chow (2014) seeks to restore to the enunciative field of Hong Kong a vibrant, pluralistic agency: it belongs to neither the Anglophone nor the Sinophone; it embodies the two and simultaneously alienates them both. On this view, the heteroglossic vernacular captures 'xenophonic memories' (p. 59). It stands outside of and remains foreign to individual named languages as bounded synchronic systems (English, Cantonese, Mandarin, and so forth), while still bearing their traces – in Jacques Derrida's sense of a path or track that points to the *absent presence* of these various named languages. In other words, postcolonial languaging is constituted by blending ingredients from various named languages, notably English and Cantonese. Yet these very languages are present only in scattered fragments and in novel combination with other elements, such that they are at the same time absent in their recognizable forms. This kind of discourse may be characterized as

> an assemblage of lived discontinuities, a network comprising what may be termed the *déjà énoncé* – the resonances, memories, associations, and affects (voluntary and involuntary) that, having been uttered and heard many times, cling to or hover around the most simple individual speech acts with a certain aura. (Chow 2021: 122)

This vantage point privileges discontinuities over continuities in the historical constitution of an enunciative field, highlighting the sustained liminality of language-in-action. As indicated in the epigraph at the beginning of this section, Chow's languaging perspective subverts the power relation between the colonizer and the colonized, and opens new doors by nullifying the perceived unity, continuity, and superiority of English native speakership as a haunting legacy of colonial rule in Hong Kong. This ties in with Li Wei's critique of the idea of English native speakership, and remedies what he describes as the English/European and monolingual biases in studies on linguistic innovation:

> The native speaker concept is inherently entangled with being monolingual, that is, to qualify as a native speaker one is assumed to be monolingual. This is not to say that 'native speakers' of English from the Inner Circles of the English-speaking world are not or cannot be bilingual or multilingual. But having languages other than English in one's repertoire, even if from birth, somehow dilutes one's competence and raises doubts over one's entitlement to the claim of a native English speaker. (Li 2020: 240)

With languaging, local ways of speaking (and we might add, of writing as well) are construable as 'xenophonic *énoncés*' (Chow 2014: 60), embedding vestiges of cultural memories and indexed as emblematic badges of singularity and difference, while constantly riffing off the former colonial language. This introduces noise into the perceived homogeneity of a literary praxis centred around a 'standard' English, or other hegemonic languages like French, Spanish, and Mandarin Chinese, thus imploding 'the illusorily unified histories of such registers' (Chow 2014: 59). In literary writing, such languaging is exemplified by Anglophone writers hailing from non-Anglophone ethnic and cultural *routes*, alluding to but theorized against *roots*, which imply vertical genealogical filiations (Hall 1996: 3). Inter alia, these writers include Salman Rushdie, Arundhati Roy, and Amitav Ghosh – and to this list we might add a growing number of English-language authors of East Asian origins publishing in the West, notably Xiaolu Guo, Yiyun Li, and Anchee Min. By drawing 'innumerable data fragments' from ethnic cultural landscapes and making 'copious references to other lingual scenarios', these writers create a transcultural niche by transforming 'the English language at their disposal into a discordant, vertiginous discourse archive' (Chow 2014: 60), thereby subverting the English-language literary establishment from within.

The present study is interested in urban linguistics, or metrolingualism,[9] rather than world literature. Yet we can take cue from Rey Chow's analytical logic to expound on the language politics of Kongish. Be it Kongish Daily or the producers of Kongish-based memorabilia, Kongish practitioners have an ambition that resonates with Anglophone writers in the likes of Rushdie, Roy, and Ghosh. To borrow Chow's words (cited above), they aim to produce a 'discordant, vertiginous discourse archive' of urban dialectal practice, through a Sinophone rearticulation of English – and, conversely, an Anglophone rearticulation of Chinese – at the disposal of Hong Kong citizen sociolinguists[10] and language marketeers.

Developing Chow's line of thinking, I want to argue that Kongish as a languaging practice is xenophonic, in that it bears the sounds (hence 'phonic') of English and Chinese at one stroke, at the same time as it alienates (hence 'xeno') both of these named languages. In invoking the notion of the Xenophone, I concurrently allude to Der-wei Wang's idea of the Xenophone which references 'the fluid, heterogeneous horizons adjacent to the Sinosphere' (Wang 2021: 316).[11] Hong Kong represents such a fluid, heterogeneous horizon

---

[9] Where metrolingualism is 'not only about the use of linguistic resources from different languages, but may equally describe those harmonizing (or sometimes parodying) practices of adjustment within codes, as well as certain forms of styling'. Metrolingualism distinguishes itself from multilingualism through its focus on 'the integration of diverse linguistic resources in the city' rather than 'the identification of specifically different codes at use at the same time', thereby questioning the underlying basis of prevailing notions of multilingualism (Pennycook & Otsuji 2015: 7).

[10] Where citizen sociolinguists refer to lay users of a particular language (who are mostly not linguistically trained, although trained linguists are not precluded either) who discuss with one another in social media about how their language is practised in their everyday lives. Citizen sociolinguistics thus represents a democratization of language studies scaled to the level of the grassroots, such that 'a diversity of viewpoints emerges, and disagreements tease out issues of genuine curiosity and concern' (Rymes 2020: 22).

[11] Der-wei Wang's Xenophone is proposed as a complementary counterpoint to the more politically oriented Sinophone studies (Shih 2011), which focuses intently on the politics of the other

within the Sinosphere, being a special administrative region on the geopolitical edges of mainland China.

Kongish, as an instantiation of xenophonic *énoncés*, therefore embodies the linguistic uncanny: it is orthographically English, frequently intercepted by calques and transliterations from Cantonese, syntactically schizophrenic, and always stranded in a grammatical no-man's land. Visually and aurally, it evokes the Anglophonic and the Sinophonic at one stroke but ultimately refuses to subscribe to either, creating *énoncés* as part of its own morphing repertoire. It borrows from but estranges the two source languages and, owing to its high multimodality, even language as such. An important clue lies in the introduction to Kongish Daily, cited above, which defines Kongish as neither Chinglish nor romanized Cantonese; and it is also not fully co-extensive with (*dou ng exactly hai*) HKE: 'Only knowing English or Cantonese ng wui give you the full picture, you have to be a Hong Konger sin can understand our page, Kongish Daily'. Indeed, even bilingual proficiency in English *and* Cantonese does not guarantee an understanding of Kongish with all its idiosyncrasies, which points to how it simultaneously encompasses and foreignizes both languages. Kongish, in other words, is innominate. And insofar as Kongish communications are not merely linguistic but multimodal, they represent a re-semiotization, a transmedial crossing, of a postcolonial audibility in Hong Kong, based on the local parole, into a *postcolonial visibility* (cf. Chow 2012: Ch. 7), as manifested in Kongish writing on social media and Kongish-based artefacts.

Kongish thus joins the ranks of related phenomena in other regions in the world, where translingual languages – or what Kellman (2020) calls 'nimble tongues' – are created out of mundane as well as creative exchanges, and mobilized by writers for identity work. Examples include Spanglish (Spanish + English), Portunhol (Portuguese + Spanish), and Frenglish (French + English) as used, for instance, by U. S. Latinx writers (África-Vidal 2022; Jones 2022); New Chinglish (Chinese + English) as used by netizens in mainland China (Li 2016); and written Singlish as used in metalinguistic Singaporean writing (Lee 2022a). From here we might press further: if, as Rey Chow (2014) contends, Anglophone writing shot through with non-Anglophone ethnocultural elements is a mode of languaging, then perhaps the propensity of Kongish as a translingual and multimodal register aligns not just with languaging, but with *trans*languaging. It is to the latter that we turn in the following section.

(namely, mainland China). For Wang (2021), the idea of the Xenophone enables us to 'investigate the formation of linguistic, cultural, and ethnic borderlands' as part of but also transcending 'nationally constructed borders and their geographically specific borderlands' (pp. 317–18). As such, the Xenophone allows us to 'critically contemplate on the "other's others", so as to render a "thick" appraisal of any given subject' (p. 316).

2 Translanguaging and Linguistic Commodification

Translanguaging has never intended to replace code-switching or any other term, although it challenges the code view of language.
– Li Wei, 'Translanguaging as a practical theory of language'

2.1 Translanguaging As a Creative-Critical Practice

If languaging evokes the 'accent, tone, texture, habit, and historicality' (Chow 2014: 65), in other words, the 'xenophonic memories' (Chow 2014: 59) of Hong Kong's vernacular, then translanguaging supplements a translingual and multimodal dimension by further emphasizing the crossings and intertextualities that transpire in bottom-up multilingualism. Translanguaging refers to the flexible deployment of resources available in a semiotic repertoire for the production of creative and critical discourses or artefacts. It has three interrelated features (Li 2011: 1223; Li 2018a: 17–18; Lee & Li 2020: 397):

a. Translanguaging involves a movement between different language systems, but also beyond language as such, fully recognizing the multimodal and multisensory nature of communication across speaking, writing, signing, listening, reading – and remembering (thus cohering with the idea of partial remembering in Rey Chow's (2014: 65) notion of languaging).

b. As with languaging, translanguaging is not just about the transmission of instrumental information, but spans an entire range of language-based, though not language-limited, performances by multilingual individuals, including the discursive construction of values, identities, and relationships.

c. Translanguaging is not restricted to textual or semiotic events; it creates holistic, transformative social spaces by converging the differential aspects of multilingual individuals' habitus (and this, again, recalls Chow's (2014: 65) embedding of habit and historicality into her notion of languaging). These aspects include their physical and cognitive characteristics; beliefs, attitudes, and ideologies; and personal histories, experiences, and environments into an orchestrated performance that gains meaning as a part of their lived experience.

As I will demonstrate below, Kongish communications encompass all of these features, creating an enunciative field for translanguaging, or a translanguaging space.[12] Whereas Kongish Daily creates an interactive platform and a community

---

[12] Where a translanguaging space is any space, material or virtual,

> where the process of what Bhabha (1994) calls 'cultural translation' between traditions takes place; it is not a space where different identities, values and practices simply co-exist,

of practice for users to playfully experiment with the xenophonic intersections of English and Cantonese, Kongish-based memorabilia commoditizes Kongish into displayable and saleable emblems of identity. As my examples in the next two sections will show, these modalities of communication cannot be sufficiently captured by the constructs of codemixing and codeswitching, for Kongish involves a more intricate transfusion and interlacing between the two (or more) named languages or codes. Befitting digital-born languages, Kongish (at least in its manifestation in Kongish Daily) also draws upon visual and symbolic resources, such as emoji, numerals, and other symbols (not to mention that intersemiotic references to images/photographs are an indispensable part of Kongish communications), hence co-opting intersemiotic modalities and transcending the medium of writing per se.

Yet the most distinctive attributes of urban dialects like Kongish rest in their 3Cs: Contingency, Creativity, and Criticality. Contingency refers to the spontaneity of Kongish communications, and it is for this reason that Kongish cannot be subject to quantitative or corpus methods in linguistics. To compute statistics on the frequencies of occurrence of certain lexical items or collocations in Kongish would be to assume from the outset that it exhibits stable lexicogrammatical patterns and constitutes a language system in itself. This latter view throws us back to the model of complementary multilingualism, premised on the parallel co-existence of different languages with delineated and stable boundaries (Li 1994: 7). Such an imaginary of multilingualism runs counter to the moment-by-moment, and at times arbitrary, whim-and-fancy nature in which Kongish writing unfolds. This characteristic aligns with what Li Wei describes as the 'spur-of-the-moment' in translanguaging, where the moment constitutes a unit of analysis defined as 'a point in or a period of time which has outstanding significance. It is characterised by its distinctiveness and impact on subsequent events or developments. People present at such moments would recognise their importance and may adjust their behaviour according to their interpretation of them' (Li 2011: 1224).

Based on this understanding of moments, Li Wei and I subsequently coined the term 'momentarity' to capture the contingency of translanguaging spaces, which are always subject to the here-and-now exigencies of communication at a particular point in time and space. Thus considered, translanguaging can be conceived as

---

but combine together to generate new identities, values and practices. The boundaries of a translanguaging space are ever-shifting; they exist primarily in the mind of the individual who creates and occupies it, and the construction of the space is an ongoing, lifelong process. (Li 2011: 1223)

a field of creative energy moving along a continuum from markedness on the one pole to unmarkedness on the other. It sets in when different features of a repertoire are spontaneously activated and converged to create temporary forms; sustains itself through the period of the perceived creativity of such forms . . . and terminates when those forms are fully embedded into everyday parlance. There is therefore *a momentarity to translanguaging*: as all creative and dynamic linguistic practices must eventually lapse into Language and become static and mundane . . . [A]ny particular instance of translanguaging is temporally finite. *Translanguaging happens in the here and now.*

(Lee & Li 2020: 413; emphasis added)

This understanding of momentarity aptly applies to Kongish, which thrives on the instantaneity of its creative communications, such as new coinage, marked collocations, and (con)fused morphologies inflecting Cantonese (an isolating language) with the rules of English grammar. We will see examples of such Kongish formations in the next section. Suffice it to say for now that these formations are transient, in that they may or may not be activated again; and even if they do recur, they do not necessarily display any regularity that can be considered statistically significant. They come and go, and occasionally return in different guises. And, as this theory goes, in the event that any such formation eventually becomes an entrenched part of the discourse over time, it will shed its novelty, its freshness if you will, in which case it will be subsumed into Language – for instance, in virtue of becoming an unmarked lexicogrammatical feature of HKE. At this point it ceases to instantiate translanguaging.

Which leads us to the attribute of creativity, which is absolutely central to any translanguaging practice. In his original formulation, Li Wei defines creativity as 'the ability to choose between following and flouting the rules and norms of behaviour, including the use of language. It is about pushing and breaking the boundaries between the old and the new, the conventional and the original, and the acceptable and the challenging' (Li 2011: 1223). More recently, Li Wei and I unpacked creativity, specifically in the context of East Asian urban dialects, as the capacity to 'hijack the orthographic form of English to subvert English *from within*' (Lee & Li 2020: 404), often to humorous effects. These practices demonstrate how a younger generation of English-language users in Sinophone regions like Hong Kong tend to 'domesticate other global dominant languages, in particular English, inflecting it with the idiosyncrasies of their local tongues and sensibilities to fashion their own brands of English' (Lee & Li 2021: 559).

The creative impulse of urban dialects like Kongish can be seen as partaking of a broader media phenomenon called the 'ludification of culture', a term proposed by the media theorist Joost Raessens. For Raessens (2014: 94), the idea of play, or the ludic,

> is not only characteristic of leisure, but also turns up in those domains that once were considered the opposite of play, such as education (e.g. educational games), politics (playful forms of campaigning, using gaming principles to involve party members in decision-making processes, comedians-turned-politicians) and even warfare (interfaces resembling computer games, the use of drones – unmanned remote-controlled planes – introducing war à la PlayStation).

Prima facie, Kongish is a ludic mode of texting among Hong Kong youths, exuding a playful resourcefulness in relation to different languages. But although it can be linguistically entertaining, Kongish is more than a faddish mode of writing: it is also a medium for social commentary. This leads us to the final attribute of criticality, defined as 'the ability to use available evidence appropriately, systematically and insightfully to inform considered views of cultural, social and linguistic phenomena, to question and problematize received wisdom, and to express views adequately through reasoned responses to situations' (Li 2011: 1223). In respect of Kongish writing, criticality is expressed through the cynical stance of its users and their sardonic response to social events, especially as regards establishment personalities or institutions. Mischievous in form and style, Kongish embodies an egalitarian ethos, seeking to critique instances of social injustice in Hong Kong and to articulate a unique voice for the Hong Kong citizenry.

On this view, Kongish represents the emergence of a *linguistic citizenship*, a concept designed 'to capture the idea that language falls firmly within citizenship discourses' (Stroud 2015: 23), hence directing critical attention to how the 'complexities and subtleties of language (just as with an appreciation for different sexualities) can initiate and sustain state remedies for more encompassing and inclusive forms of citizenship agency and participation' (Stroud 2015: 24). Unlike HKE, Kongish does not ensue from cumulative practices of language contact; it is a consciously crafted, civic-oriented urban dialect that 'recognizes that speakers express agency, voice and participation through a variety of semiotic means', instantiating claims 'for new forms of inclusion by using their language over many modalities' (Stroud 2015: 25).

What ensues from translanguaging practices like Kongish communications, then, is not multilingualism understood as the simple co-existence of diverse languages – complementary multilingualism – but as 'a rich source of creativity and criticality, as it entails tension, conflict, competition, difference, change in a number of spheres, ranging from ideologies, policies and practices to historical and current contexts' (Li 2011: 1223–4). And because this playful mode of multilingualism is still in the making, not least in East Asian cities like Hong Kong, it may well be described as a 'utopian multilingualism' articulating an ideal, hence utopic, conception of language that 'goes hand in glove with a euphoric, embodied and new sense of self' (Stroud & Williams 2017: 178). This connects directly to what Stroud and Williams describe as multilingualism as utopia, where a register is developed to *talk about (multilingual) talk*, and to engage with 'how language emerge[s], uneasily or easily, out of encounters across difference' (Stroud & Williams 2017: 185). Language, as it were, becomes more than language. It integrates into the multisensory embodiment and continual transformation of identities. This entails a reconceptualization of language as 'a formative dynamic in encounters [which] promises to widen our understanding of the complexities and contextualities of the notion of multilingualism itself. … [I]t focuses our attention on multilingualism as a site where language and self can be refashioned through practical engagement with how encounters are semiotized' (Stroud & Williams 2017: 185).

Kongish, therefore, should not be understood merely as a variety of English with Hong Kong characteristics – namely HKE. It is rather a more pointed medium for the ludic articulation of a vernacular-based community of practice, signalling a burgeoning linguistic citizenship among Hong Kong youths, based around a utopian idea of multilingualism through translanguaging.

2.2 Commodifying Urban Dialects: From Social Media Writing to Text-Based Artefacts

We have now established that translanguaging is a translingual and multimodal practice that is contingent, creative, and critical. The next question that arises is the platform(s) on which translanguaging practices are performed, which has to do with the mediality of the communications in question. It is at this juncture that the idea of commodification becomes useful to us as a rubric for understanding how language participates within urban economies.

The commodification of language as a sociolinguistic phenomenon has been understood in different ways. From a sociological perspective, language can be conceived as a resource with exchange value in the marketplace and developed as part of one's capital in a sociological (Bourdieusian) sense. What is of interest to this approach is how language participates in the generation of value under the conditions of late capitalism and high modernity. Heller (2010: 103; see also 104–5) maintains that language gains a new importance in the globalized economy by

a. 'managing the flow of resources over extended spatial relations and compressed space-time relations', as global capitalist ventures transcending geographical borders necessitate the management of linguistic differences in communication;

b. 'providing symbolic added value to industrially produced resources', as the automation of industrial processes demands new modes and degrees of literacy in, say, technical jargon or programming language;

c. 'developing linguistically mediated knowledge and service industries', such as in call-centres where service consultants are trained to speak in a standardized English discourse cleansed of local accents to cater to a global clientele; and

d. 'facilitating the construction of and access to niche markets', especially in the tourism industry where language gains an emblematic value indexing cultural authenticity, which translates into added economic value for touristy collectibles.

One crucial theme in Heller's work is the tension between language-as-identity and language-as-skill, 'both of which are commodifiable in the globalized new economy' (Heller 2010: 103). This theme finds resonance in Lionel Wee's work on Singlish as it is commodified. Here, one may distinguish between two conceptions of commodification, namely (Wee 2018: 118–40):

a. the Marxist notion of commodity as that which is extrinsic to the individual, and

b. the neoliberal understanding of commodity as that which constitutes one's human capital and is hence inalienable from an individual's capacity development.

According to Wee (2018), the so-called culture industries in Singapore – theatrical, film, fictional, or lexicographical productions ventriloquizing Singlish as a local tongue – tend to draw on the Marxist notion. These productions construct Singlish as 'an independently existing object, one that can be bought and sold' (p. 123), thereby turning Singlish competence into a marketable resource. Here, the Singlish commodities in question derive their 'imprimatur of authenticity' (p. 134) from their producers' (presumed or claimed) identity as Singlish native speakers – a notion that needs critical questioning.[13] By contrast, the so-called non-culture industries – for instance, foreign expatriates in Singapore producing YouTube videos to teach Singlish to other expatriates, attracting virtual or material rewards

---

[13] Here, Wee (2018: 138) makes the qualification that the connections between language-as-commodity and native speakership is not inherent to Marxist theory: 'But as a matter of historical default, the traditional influence of Marx's view of commodification and the tendency to think of language as a bounded autonomous system about which native speakers have some special intuition or knowledge have converged'.

such as subscriptions and 'likes' – tap into the neoliberal view of commodities. Here, urban dialects like Singlish are perceived as a skill-form that all individuals, native to Singapore or not, can acquire to varying degrees of proficiency as part of their linguistic repertoire and personal capacity development.

With this in view, the present study adopts a two-pronged approach to the commodification of Kongish. The first corresponds to what Wee (2018: 134) describes as the use of the vernacular as an 'imprimatur of authenticity', or what Heller (2010: 103) identifies as language-as-identity: 'expressions of true selves or of relatively good or poor accomplishments of socially located personae'. Note, however, that the idea of language-as-identity is construed in this study not as referencing the use of language as an anchor for consolidating macro-identities or traditional regimes of discursive authenticity based around the nation-state, but, on the contrary, as the distribution of bottom-up identities based around the fluid formation of translingual urban dialects. For this, I use Kongish Daily as a case study to exemplify how Hong Kong netizens ride on the affordances of Facebook to experiment with the creative interplay among English, Cantonese, as well as myriad visual modalities of instantaneous texting to co-create a translanguaging space on social media. I will show that this mode of Kongish writing is based not just on a locale-specific knowledge of the urban dialect, but also on an intimate familiarity with the customs and conventions of contemporary Hong Kong society.

My second approach corresponds to what Wee (2018) describes as the neo-liberal conception of linguistic commodification, where language is seen as a set of resources available for consumption by all persons, not just to the so-called native speakers. This is also what Heller (2010: 103) calls language-as-skill, which construes language as marketable items, 'producing late capitalist subjec-tivities' particularly in the context of developing niche markets in the tourism industry. As I will elaborate in the section on Kongish-based collectibles, these niche markets are commercial ventures using locale-specific identities as their value proposition, with an eye to selling text-based, tourist-oriented memorabilia featuring the urban dialect as part of their making and marketing. In this case, Kongish becomes a value-adding resource to everyday commodities like bever-ages and T-shirts by affording them a symbolic identity through vernacular epithets evocative of a grassroots affect. To distinguish this language-as-skill type of commodification in the marketplace from the language-as-identity type in Kongish Daily, I will refer to it as *commoditization*.

2.3 The Commodity Situation and Enregisterment of Kongish

We need to pause here for a moment and ask: how did Kongish, assuming it traces its initial roots to HKE, come to acquire the felicitous conditions for commodification in the first place? In the terms developed by Arjun Appadurai (1986), one needs to map out the *commodity situation* in the social trajectory of Kongish, where the commodity situation of a thing is defined as 'the situation in which its exchangeability (past, present, or future) for some other thing is its socially relevant feature' (p. 13). Answering this question requires looking at how features associated with English as it is used in Hong Kong – leaving aside for the moment the terminological issues around HKE versus Kongish – have attracted different meanings over time in the particular sociocultural time-spaces of the city.

2.3.1 The Commodity Phase

According to Appadurai (1986), the first element in a commodity situation is the Commodity Phase. Applying this to the case at hand, this refers to the set of ideas that local people in Hong Kong have developed around vernacular speech giving it the potential to be commodified as a niche medium for social media communication and as a sellable product (see Johnstone 2009: 162). Taking cue from Johnstone's (2009: 162–4) seminal study of Pittsburghese, the 'imagined' urban dialect of Pittsburgh (see also Johnstone et al. 2006),[14] I will have recourse to Silverstein's (2003) notion of 'orders of indexicality' as a framework to attempt a mapping of the stages through which Kongish as we know it today is *enregistered* (Agha 2003, 2007), where its features are imbued with a valuation invoking grassroots literacy (Blommaert 2008) and a recalcitrant ethos.

In Silverstein's (2003) scheme, nth-order indexicality, reworked by Johnstone (2009) as 'first-order' indexicality, refers to a stage where linguistic features of a certain language become 'hearable' – that is, perceived to be distinctive – as related to the sociodemographic facts about its users. Such correlation may be established by, for instance, linguists using taxonomies of features gathered from fieldwork to distinguish a locally variant or 'dialectal' way of speaking with reference to an assumed standard core of language. Applying this to Hong Kong's case, HKE has long been identified by linguists

---

[14] Johnstone et al. (2006) trace the birth and evolution of Pittsburghese, an 'imagined dialect' embodying speech features that have come to be associated with a regional locale (southwestern Pennsylvania, especially Pittsburgh). Through the process of enregisterment (Agha 2003, 2007), these speech features codify into an index of locale-specific identity ('Pittsburgher') which the speakers themselves can invoke to do social identity work ('I am [not] a Pittsburgher'). Once this indexical link between Pittsburghese speech forms and a Pittsburgh identity becomes reified, it lends itself to creative performance (Bauman & Briggs 1990), whereby Pittsburghers as well as non-Pittsburghers 'use regional forms drawn from highly codified lists to perform local identity, often in ironic, semiserious ways' (Johnstone et al. 2006: 83). And it is when an urban dialect reaches this last stage called third-order indexicality (Johnstone et al. 2006, drawing on Silverstein 2003) that it gets commodified, for instance, into Pittsburghese shirts. See my discussion later with reference to Table 1.

as a distinctive variety of English. Notably, Bolton (2002b: 44–51), based on Butler's (1997) criteria for World Englishes, has established HKE's status as a legitimate variety of English by demonstrating its characteristics, as follows (elaborations in square parentheses are mine):

a. A Hong Kong accent characterized by segmental and supra-segmental phonological features, shared and recognized by speakers of English in Hong Kong (see Bolton & Kwok 1990; Luk 1998);

b. A distinct Hong Kong vocabulary, as reported in academic studies and evidenced by the inclusion of Hong Kong words in lexicographical projects on Asian Englishes. [As mentioned earlier, it is noteworthy that, in 2016, the *OED* included several loanwords transliterated or calqued from Cantonese, attesting to the visibility of the HKE lexicon.];

c. A history of language contact that undergirds the distinctive features of HKE, going back to the seventeenth century and interacting with the colonial history (since 1842) and postcolonial dynamics (post-1997) of Hong Kong (Bolton 2002b: 31–35; see also Poon 2010; see Bolton 2011 for an updated review). [And I would later argue that this historical development now culminates in Kongish, which is ontologically borne out of HKE, but exceeds the latter in terms of its contingency, creativity, and criticality.];

d. A corpus of English-language literary works by Hong Kong writers such as Xu Xi and Louise Ho [although it must be pointed out that the literary practices identified by Bolton (2002b: 48) are not exclusively or even primarily based around HKE, even if they are inflected by the cultural sensibilities of Hong Kong];

e. Reference works that acknowledge HKE as a variety of English. [Bolton uses as his example the Hong Kong section of the ICE database. A more recent example would be *A Dictionary of Hong Kong English* (Cummings and Wolf 2011) published by Hong Kong University Press, mentioned in the previous section.]

To this list, we can add more recent scholarship (and no doubt there will be even more in the future) that espouses HKE as a distinctive variety of English, including Wong's (2017) work on lexicogrammatical and discourse features, cited earlier.

The identification of HKE's distinctive features by linguists establishes these features as a first-order indexical by construing them as place-based, that is, made-in-Hong Kong. Now when these features become hearable not just to linguists but to local users of English themselves, we move from what Silverstein (2003) describes as the nth-order to n+1-th-order of indexicality, or what Johnstone (2009) translates as 'second-order' indexicality. This is where features of HKE become noticeable to local persons, perhaps due to their frequent contact and contrast with so-called native speakers of English, as a marker of class or correctness. This is evidenced in surveys that have shown a range of attitudes among local Hong Kong people toward HKE, ranging from stigmatization to acceptance. On the one end, HKE is seen as a non-native offshoot of British English, pointing to the territory's colonial history and, more particularly, the relatively less cosmopolitan background of its users. On the other end, it marks an affective belonging to Hong Kong. According to Hansen Edward's (2015) study, a slight majority of her respondents concurred that HKE is an identifiable variety representing English as it is spoken in Hong Kong (p. 202); that English has 'symbolic value in portraying a Hong Kong identity in post-handover Hong Kong'; and that it is 'HKE, and not an "exonormative" model of English, [that] plays this role for some speakers of English in Hong Kong' (p. 206). This shows that the sociocultural conditions are in place for local people to activate resources from HKE to foreground – or not – their class and/or locale orientation, pointing to the enregisterment of HKE as a second-order indexical.

Importantly, however, it is found that only a minority of respondents recognized HKE as 'a legitimate variety or as good as other varieties of English' (p. 202). Using Kachru's (1983) notion of linguistic schizophrenia, Hansen Edwards (2015: 202; emphasis added) opines that Hong Kong speakers of English

> appear to be conflicted about their feelings towards HKE – on the one hand, they acknowledge its existence and its representation of Hong Kong identity and culture, but on the other, they *do not want to speak it*, preferring 'native' exonormative models or varieties over HKE and *often judging it negatively* in comparison to exonormative varieties such as BrE [British English] and AmE [American English].

Hansen Edwards's surveys were conducted in October 2014. As she notes, her findings offer a 'snapshot' of HKE's status in Hong Kong at that particular point in time (p. 206). And 2014 also happened to be a threshold year for the city, the year when Occupy Central (also known as the Umbrella Movement) took place, leading on to more radicalized social movements in the subsequent years. The rest, as it is often said, is history.

I venture to speculate that it is at this juncture, in the vicinity of the year 2014, that Kongish entered the picture, transitioning away from HKE's schizophrenic disposition and enregistering itself as a reflexive medium for identity work. In this regard, it is not coincidental that the Facebook page Kongish Daily was inaugurated in 2015, in the aftermath of Occupy Central, and that the commoditization of Kongish in the commercial market also became much more aggressive within the same period. In other words, recent developments in the local socio-political scene post-2014 may have triggered an ever-more heightened awareness of HKE features as signifiers of Hong Kong's cultural identity, leading to subtle shifts toward the acceptance as opposed to the stigmatization pole (see also Sewell & Chan 2016).

Indeed, in her follow-up study to investigate the language attitudes of HKE speakers pre- and post-Umbrella Movement, Hansen Edwards (2016: 163) finds that 'there have been substantial changes in how HKE is viewed by the population surveyed', with statistics indicating an increased acceptance of HKE among local users and a greater propensity to embody a so-called Hong Kong identity. There is therefore a strong correlation between enhanced attitudes toward HKE among the local populace and their enhanced awareness of a place-based identity, although it is unclear whether this can be attributed solely to particular socio-political events or whether it is 'merely a reflection of the changing linguistic and political landscape of Hong Kong' (p. 163).

Regardless of the underlying reason, this shift in language attitudes may have created the impetus for HKE to be tipped toward Silverstein's (n+1)+1-th-order indexicality, which Johnstone (2009) construes as 'third-order' indexicality. This is where local users of English in Hong Kong consciously appropriate its features, often in an apparently non-serious manner, to perform a locale-specific cultural identity. In this connection, it is noteworthy that a 2016 *SCMP* commentary hailed Kongish as a language borne out of the Occupy protests,[15] while another 2019 article on *SCMP*'s Post Magazine brands it as a language of 'empowerment' in the social movement context.[16] This indicates a potential correlation between the emergence of Kongish and the consolidation of critical sociopolitical sentiments. Such a correlation is precisely enregisterment: the valuation of an urban dialect with a particular stance.

Here I want to reiterate my conjecture – that this is the point where the urban dialect of Kongish may have evolved out of HKE without, however, displacing the latter. At this stage, not only are HKE features de-stigmatized as symptoms of second-language or foreign-language speakership, they are enregistered and re-semiotized into a *sui generis* medium that subverts English from within by translanguaging it with resources from the Chinese languages, primarily

---

[15] https://www.scmp.com/lifestyle/article/1903452/hongkongers-mix-english-and-cantonese-new-language-kongish?module=perpetual_scroll_0&pgtype=article&campaign=1903452;.

[16] https://www.scmp.com/magazines/post-magazine/short-reads/article/3024863/do-you-speak-kongish-hong-kong-protesters?module=perpetual_scroll_0&pgtype=article&campaign=3024863.

Cantonese (through calques or transliterations), *and* with other symbolic resources, such as numbers and emojis (see Li et al. 2020). The result is a unique discursive concoction that transgresses the boundaries between named languages and extends beyond language as such, designed to resist any easy comprehension by non-local users of English.

As with Pittsburghese, it is at this third indexical order, when local linguistic forms are 'no longer linked exclusively with class or correctness but also (or, for some people, instead) with local identity' (Johnstone 2009: 163), that Kongish enters the commodity phase. It then becomes commodifiable as a niche communicative medium and marketable product. To borrow Johnstone's (2009: 163) language, substituting Kongish for Pittsburgh(ese):

> It is at this stage [the third indexical order] that a Kongish word or phrase can come to evoke local pride or nostalgia, even among people who do not identify themselves as working-class or as speakers of a nonstandard variety. While the earlier (and, for some people, still exclusively) more stigmatized meanings of local forms still resonate, so that a Kongish shirt may still call to mind working-class pride and disregard for correctness, this link is now indirect, mediated by the association of local forms with authentic localness.

The empirical evidence for this third-indexical order usage of English in Hong Kong will be presented in the next two sections on Kongish Daily and Kongish-based commodities respectively. For now, it suffices to say that Kongish has in recent years entered the commodity phase through its enregisterment as a third-order indexical. Table 1 summarizes the various indexical orders speculated to have been moved through by HKE/Kongish, by analogy to the trajectory of Pittsburghese (Johnstone 2009).

2.3.2 Commodity Candidacy and Commodity Context

According to Arjun Appadurai, the commodity situation of an entity, having entered the commodity phase, entails two other aspects. These are Commodity Candidacy – the 'cultural framework', the 'standards and criteria (symbolic, classificatory, and moral) that define the exchangeability of things in any particular social and historical context' (Appadurai 1986: 14) – and Commodity Context – 'the variety of *social* arenas, within or between *cultural* units, that help link the commodity candidacy of a thing to the commodity phase of its career' (Appadurai 1986: 15).

Once again, Johnstone's analysis of Pittsburghese in commodification within Appadurai's framework provides a good point of reference for us. In respect of commodity candidacy, Johnstone (2009) focuses on the ideology of *folklorism* that valorizes traditional, longstanding, and place-based folk practices, including

Table 1. Indexical orders and the transition from HKE to Kongish

Silverstein (2003)/Johnstone (2009)	HKE/Kongish
Nth-order indexical Linguistic features become hearable – by linguists, not local users – as distinctive of particular locales and correlated to sociodemographic facts (e.g., place of origin) of language users.	**First-order indexicality** Features of speech are isolated by linguists and correlated to Hong Kong as their point of origin and distinction, leading to the notion of HKE as a variety of World/Asian/Postcolonial Englishes.
N+1-th-order indexicality Linguistic features are associated with values of class or correctness by local speakers themselves, often with reference to an exonormative standard, such as Received Pronunciation. Having recognized this correlation, local persons can appropriate features associated with local usage to highlight, or not, their identity as belonging to a certain locale and/or class (e.g., as working-class men from Pittsburgh).	**Second-order indexicality** Features associated with HKE, identified on the first indexical order, become perceivable by Hong Kong users of English themselves and enregistered as non-native and/or substandard vis-à-vis British English, or, alternatively, as connoting a heartlander (versus metropolitan) identity. These features may be activated by highly proficient users to either foreground or suppress their locale-specific identity.
(N+1)+1-th-order indexicality Linguistic features gain a new, possibly more positive, interpretation when seen through the lens of a different ideological schema, such as one correlating nonstandard, dialectal usage to authentic local identity and an ironic, semi-serious stance.	**Third-order indexicality** Features associated with HKE are enregistered as badges of a Hong Kong cultural identity and are re-semiotized into the written medium of Kongish and multimodally commodified through, for instance, Kongish Daily and Kongish-based artefacts for sale. Such commodification is often infused with a reflexive playfulness.

linguistic practices (p. 164). Folklorism is tied to the notion of cultural authenticity, which in turn is connected to the idea of 'place' in the cultural geographical sense (Cresswell 2014). Thus, in Pittsburgh, the display of local speech, such as on T-shirts, 'is sometimes part and parcel of the display of other elements of local cultural heritage, like steelworkers' hard hats, plaques and signs commemorating local people and historical moments, buildings where memorable events occurred, and the like' (Johnstone 2009: 165). The locale-specificity of linguistic forms therefore comes to index an imagined, place-based authenticity.

Turning to Hong Kong, recent years have witnessed a proliferation of books and social media resources on folk etymologies in relation to Cantonese, customary traditions from yesteryear Hong Kong, historical anecdotes around the city's street names and personages, and other similar themes. A cursory look at the Hong Kong section in two major bookstore chains in the city, Commercial Press and Joint Publishing, yields an abundance of relevant examples. For instance, the publisher Enlighten and Fish,[17] in collaboration with the Facebook page Cantonese Museum,[18] produced a series of Chinese-language books curated around Cantonese and Hong Kong, such as Cantonese primers designed in the form of traditional Chinese almanacs; compendia of Cantonese idioms; introductions to Hong Kong's culture and customs through Cantonese vocabulary; and anthologies of legends and 'strange tales' from Hong Kong. Other products put out by different publishers include stories about less well-known historical individuals, literary memoirs on Hong Kong, collections of old advertisements from local newspapers, and picture books like *Milktealogy* – a neologism based on a local milk tea beverage – on vernacular food in the ubiquitous *cha chaan teng* (literally, 'tea-food cafe').[19]

These resources are unrelated to Kongish per se, but they speak to a cultural framework in Hong Kong construed around the ethnographic intricacies of Cantonese and its associated tradition. Particularly symptomatic of this framework is the virtual Cantonese Museum, which on its Facebook page introduces Cantonese as a heritage language embodied in traditional Cantonese opera, oral performance cultures, children's jingles, indigenous songs, and with a diasporic presence in Chinese descendent communities in Southeast Asia, Australia, and North America.[20] The museum also maintains a YouTube channel uploaded with videos on Cantonese etymologies and popular culture (think Bruce Lee).[21] These examples instantiate a folklorism that connects language, cultural authenticity, and place-based identity. It is the development of this framework, especially in the contemporary context of Hong Kong's identity flux and crisis, that gives Kongish its commodity candidacy as an urban dialect – in other words, its sociocultural currency for commodification into an identity emblem.

---

[17] https://www.facebook.com/enlightenfish.
[18] https://www.facebook.com/CantoneseMuseum.
[19] For a full range of titles, see the catalogue of the online bookstore https://www.signer.com.hk.
[20] https://www.facebook.com/CantoneseMuseum/.
[21] https://www.youtube.com/c/CantoneseMuseum廣東話資料館.

Finally, commodity context refers to the technical and economic factors that facilitate the commodification of a language (Johnstone 2009: 165). In Hong Kong, there is a readily available appetite for the consumption of Kongish as both a youth dialect and a marketable product. Internet and social media penetration in Hong Kong are extremely high. An official report by Hong Kong's Legislative Council evidences an increase in the popularity of social media in terms of both participation rates and the number of hours spent on relevant platforms, especially among youngsters.[22] Recent statistics indicate that there were 6.68 million social media users in the city in January 2022, amounting to 88.1 per cent of the total population.[23] All of this creates the felicitous technical condition for the increasing popularity of Kongish as a social media-based urban slang.

As one of the most affluent cities and popular tourist destinations in Asia, Hong Kong has long developed an industry around local brands and memorabilia. The rise of Kongish-based businesses and artefacts is grounded on both the demand for such products and the sociocultural maturation of the urban dialect into a consumable – a phenomenon also attested in comparable multilingual cities like Singapore (see Lee 2022a: Ch. 6). Johnstone (2009: 165–6) further mentions the need for linguistic elements and design ideas to be available in order for urban dialects like Pittsburghese to be commoditized on everyday items like T-shirts. As Lisa Lim points out, since the end of the twentieth century, 'young Hongkongers – in internet chat rooms, text messages and on social media – have been romanising Cantonese for greater efficacy'.[24] The increasing popularity of romanized Cantonese has provided the requisite resource for Kongish-based commodities, which furthermore draw on visual motifs relating to vernacular Hong Kong culture. This phenomenon will be dealt with in greater detail in Section 4 on commoditization.

2.4 Interim Summary and Methodological Note

Before we proceed with the case studies, it may be apt to summarize the basic tenets of the present study. Using the lens of translanguaging, I aim to sketch a semiotic profile of Kongish as an emerging urban dialect in contemporary Hong Kong, focusing on how it communicates a ludic, transgressive voice from below. Playfulness is key to Kongish. The following two sections will each focus on one medium for such communications. I will first examine the

---

[22] https://www.legco.gov.hk/research-publications/english/1920issh15-social-media-usage-in-hong-kong-20191212-e.pdf.

[23] https://datareportal.com/reports/digital-2022-hong-kong.

[24] https://www.scmp.com/magazines/post-magazine/short-reads/article/3024863/do-you-speak-kongish-hong-kong-protesters?module=perpetual_scroll_0&pgtype=article&campaign=3024863.

Facebook page Kongish Daily using the method of close reading to tease out the intersections between diverse linguistic and extralinguistic resources based on the Hong Kong vernacular and the multimodal functionalities of Facebook. We will then move on to the realm of text-based artefacts, where Kongish becomes a central resource in what Kelly-Holmes (2020) calls 'the linguistic business of marketing'. Using examples from Hong Kong-based businesses such as *Gweilo*, *Fok Hing Gin*, and *Goods of Desire*, I will demonstrate how Kongish is not simply an urban dialect shared among a relatively small community of social media users obsessed with the vernacular and the local. It is *in itself* a marketable commodity participating within the neoliberal conception of language as a mobile resource for conviviality, and fully embedded within capitalist entrepreneurial practices revolving around place-based nostalgia.

Together, the two case studies give us an initial picture of Kongish as it is evolving at this point in time in Hong Kong's semiotic landscape. Dovetailing with Rey Chow's idea of the Xenophone, the ensuing discussion aims to supplement a cultural studies angle to the current conversation around Kongish, arguing that the hybrid urban dialect is neither Anglophonic nor Sinophonic. It is Xenophonic: it eschews obvious *roots* in named languages to establish new *routes* across normative borders, extending our imaginary of urban multilingualism in late modernity toward the post-multilingual (Li 2018b; Lee 2022a) and the liquid-modern (Bauman 2000).

A note on methodology is in order. I have earlier explained the idea of momentarity in relation to translanguaging. Although the term is conceived in the context of naturally occurring spoken interactions, there is no reason why momentarity cannot be extended to written environments to spotlight singular instances of creative and critical interventions, whereby linguistic resources are flexibly and contingently deployed by the seat of one's pants, without regard to institutionalized patterns that govern normative usage. Recall that the focus of moment analysis is on 'spontaneous, impromptu, and momentary actions and performances of the individual' (Li 2011: 1224) – in our case, the Kongish Daily editors who author the posts on their webpage.[25] As with what Maher (2010) calls metrolinguistic play, Kongish is not an institutionalized code and stable repertoire (as yet); it is rather 'employed as a form of on-the-spot knowledge' (p. 578), and continually negotiated by Kongish Daily editors and their followers as it is being enunciated and experimented with.

Therefore, although I have collected what can be called a 'corpus' of Kongish Daily posts, the methodology undergirding this study is diametrically opposed

---

[25] As far as Kongish Daily is concerned, this study looks only at the postings put up by its editors and not the comments by the page's followers in response to these postings. The latter topic deserves a separate study using a participatory linguistics framework.

to corpus-based research with all its emphasis on quantification and generalization. As Coupland (2007: 9) maintains in respect of variationist sociolinguistics, quantitative methods, while completely legitimate in social scientific research, represent 'an abstraction away from the social process of speaking and of making meaning in context'; the latter instead prioritizes 'looking at language variation in its primary ecosystem of discursive meaning'. By the same token, rather than the systematicity and generality typically associated with quantitative analysis, moment analysis places a premium on particularity and transitoriness, where the frequency and patterns of occurrence of specific tokens are less relevant considerations and of little purchase. In this regard, Li Wei (2022) challenges the ideas of systematicity and reproducibility in applied linguistic approaches to everyday moments of interaction. In the age of big data and neat metrics, these moments are easily dismissed as small, hence insignificant, data. But it is precisely the latter type of data that can give us insight into the personal experience of language users, and the nuances of such experience can hardly be objectified. To capture the spontaneity of translanguaging practices, one should instead appeal to the most basic of methods, namely Looking, Listening, Talking, and Thinking (LLTT), typically framed by linguistic anthropologists as ethnographic methods.

These methodological observations are relevant to the case at hand. As an experimental register still in flux, Kongish is best captured, through the lens of translanguaging, as singular moments rather than systemic patterns. Indeed, it is counterproductive, if not outright paradoxical, to approach performative urban dialects like Kongish as if it were a codified, named language with discrete and countable features. This is not to say that Kongish exhibits no distinctive features at all. Rather, whatever features attendant to Kongish must be seen as emerging contingently within a fluid and amorphous repertoire. Many of these features belong to what David Crystal calls 'textese', the use of which, according to Crystal (2010: 193), indicates linguistic creativity. And I would add that to be linguistically creative means to always maintain a tinge of newness. Newness necessarily elides objectification, for only stable linguistic features can be meaningfully subject to quantification.

A repertoire such as Kongish would thus be resistant to, for instance, coding procedures. Once we start coding Kongish writing for patterns, we would have made the mistake of taking the register 'too seriously', so to speak, with the assumption that it is already a settled code offering itself up to be theoretically framed and clinically analysed. This self-seriousness on the part of the researcher contradicts the (im)provisional and ludic nature of Kongish, whose linguistic energies derive from playful translingual coinage and slippage that speak to 'a constructivist here-and-now' (Maher 2010: 577). Not to mention that the inherent multimodality of Kongish communications means much of it would elide linguistic quantification: to count the number of 'smiley' emoticons in Kongish writing, as opposed to 'heart' emoticons, for instance, would be quite insensible from a methodological point of view.

The upshot of all this is the recognition that Kongish is not (yet) a *thing* which we can definitively put a finger on. It exists through partaking of a holistic practice driven by the imperatives of social media or marketing communications, where its participants creatively experiment with a grassroots literacy in expressing critical perspectives on everyday events – or, as the case may be, in marketing text-based products. To understand Kongish-as-praxis, we need to look into its 'moments' as they unfold within their 'primary ecosystem of discursive meaning' (Coupland 2007: 9), namely Kongish Daily's Facebook page and the market of place-based merchandise. In contradistinction to systemic methods, therefore, my analysis is largely anecdotal (see Lee 2022b; Li 2022), aimed at capturing the episodic and punctuative qualities of Kongish discourse, without purporting to exhaustively represent its repertoire – an impossibility, since that repertoire is still in the making. By way of close reading the linguistics and semiotics of Kongish Daily posts and Kongish-based artefacts, I seek to arrest moments that exemplify the Xenophonic affect of Kongish; that is: how it inflects the Anglophone with the Sinophone (and vice versa), the linguistic with the semiotic, in positioning itself as a translational Other.

Close reading as a method will always involve a measure of subjectivity, which is fully in line with the ethos of moment analysis, as discussed above. And this is where I should clarify my positionality as a researcher of Kongish in this study. As a Singaporean based in Hong Kong for more than a decade, I am kind of an insider-outsider with respect to Kongish. While I have intermediate proficiency in Cantonese, I am not privy to all the allusions and nuances in Kongish communications. Indeed, there are occasions where I find myself unable to understand a posting on Kongish Daily or an epithet on a Kongish T-shirt at all, and in these instances, I would consult a research assistant in order to get a handle on it. This need not be seen as a weakness; on the contrary, my highly personal and mildly (not fully) estranged encounter with Kongish only points to its Xenophonic quality. The condition of being stranded in the liminal zone between comprehension and incomprehension is itself meaningful, for it embeds me as an involved (and at times confused) reader of Kongish, allowing me to engage with the urban dialect *experientially*. To experience Kongish as an insider-outsider compels me to work through it with extra cognitive-perceptual effort, and this learning process becomes part of the research itself. At times, I might even be reading my own interpretation into a piece of Kongish communication which may not have been intended by its author or fathomed by local readers. Such misreading, as I will argue later, is idiosyncratic but legitimate, as it evidences the porousness of Kongish as a continually evolving and open-ended register.

3 Kongish Daily: Translanguaging on Facebook

If you want to learn English, Sor(9)ly, this site ng wui help you learn more English, but to share news with you in Kongish, finish.

– Kongish Daily

3.1 Kongish Daily As a Discourse Event

Shortly after Kongish Daily was inaugurated on Facebook on 3 August 2015, it was hailed on an internet news forum as 'Hong Kong's hottest new Facebook page',[26] reportedly gaining between 10,000 and 15,000 'likes' within twenty-four hours of its inception (Li et al. 2020: 309). The Facebook page has since received considerable press coverage and popular attention, with more than 74,000 followers and in excess of 70,000 'likes' at the time of this writing. It has even been lauded as 'an important discourse event' in Hong Kong (Lee & Li 2020: 402). Kongish Daily can therefore be said to have sent ripples through Hong Kong's mediascape.[27]

Kongish Daily was set up by three English-language lecturers in Hong Kong who go by the appellation 'little editors' – the latter word often deliberately (mis)spelled *editers*. The latter phrase is calqued from the colloquial Chinese *xiaobian* 小編 referring to people who manage webpages by way of posting updates and responding to public comments. Although Kongish Daily is technically a news-sharing page, it does not aim at a 'straight' reportage of local happenings. Rather, it is a critical forum where the editors deliver ludic, punchy postings expressing a grassroots, egalitarian stance for the consumption and feedback of their followers on Facebook.

---

[26] https://coconuts.co/hongkong/news/kongish-daily-hong-kongs-hottest-new-facebook-page/.

[27] For Appadurai, mediascapes are one of the five dimensions comprising global cultural flows, along with ethnoscapes, technoscapes, finanscapes, and ideoscapes. Of importance is what Appadurai says about the suffix '-scape': the *scapes* 'are not objectively given relations which look the same from every angle of vision, but rather ... are deeply perspectival constructs, inflected very much by the historical, linguistic, and political situatedness of different sorts of actors: nation-states, multinationals, diasporic communities ... and even intimate face-to-face groups, such as villages, neighbourhoods and families' (Appadurai 1990: 296). My positioning of Kongish Daily as part of Hong Kong's mediascape points to its historical, linguistic, and political situatedness as a community of vernacular praxis among multilingual netizens (Appadurai's 'actors') within Hong Kong's global media ecology.

Editorial postings in Kongish Daily are typically short, ranging from a single phrase to a series of sentences; they are almost always complemented by annotated images taken from local newspapers or other web portals, and often hyperlinked to particular news stories. The posts are written in a register which, at first blush, resembles a version of creolized English, hence the term Kongish. As discussed in the previous sections, Kongish is genealogically related to HKE but formally distinguished from it – and from English in general, and (more controversially) even from language as such. Here the discourse in Kongish Daily exhibits different tendencies in terms of what one might tentatively call grammatical felicity. Some postings are written in a relatively well-formed English, punctuated with calques or transliterations of Cantonese expressions in varying degrees; others border on unintelligibility, where the dosage of romanized Cantonese is so high that one is hard pressed to call the writing English at all.

As seen in the introduction to the page, cited in Section 1, Kongish Daily takes on a metadiscursive agenda; that is, to look into how local people use English in iconoclastic ways – *The site is founded bcoz we want to collect relly research how people say Kongish by looking at everyone ge replies* ('The site is founded because we want to collect real research [data on] how people speak Kongish by looking at everyone's replies'). This raises the question of what Kongish looks like in more concrete formations, which is the objective of the present section.

Apart from HKE, Kongish is affiliated to but differentiated from yet another variety, namely Chinglish. As we saw in Kongish Daily's mission statement in Section 1, the editors of Kongish affirm from the outset that Kongish *ng hai exac7ly Chinglish* ('Kongish is not exactly Chinglish'), and that one of the aims of the Facebook page is to change the commonplace idea that *Chinglish = Kongish* ('Chinglish is the equivalent of Kongish'), while at the same time distancing itself from HKE and positioning itself beyond mere romanized Cantonese. This emphatic differentiation with Chinglish on the part of the pioneers of Kongish Daily is in line with Victor Mair's remarks on the relation between Kongish and Chinglish:

> I suppose that some might wish to refer to Kongish as a topolect of Chinglish. In truth, though, Kongish is more coherent and integral than Chinglish. Chinglish is more amorphous and doesn't really have any rules. Everything in Chinglish is pretty much ad hoc and spontaneous (anything goes), whereas Kongish – *because Hong Kongers have been developing it for decades and are apt to actually exchange whole sentences and even series of sentences in it* – has a body of *mutually agreed upon usages and a higher degree of intelligibility for its own speakers*. In this sense, it resembles Singlish

(Singaporean English) more than Chinglish. Perhaps we may say that Kongish and Singlish are both *lects* of English, and that Chinglish is a work that is forever in progress.[28]

Mair is right in saying that Kongish is more 'coherent and integral' than Chinglish. The latter denotes a type of malformed English translated from the Chinese language by translation programs or by persons with limited proficiency in English. (Compare New Chinglish, an urban dialect circulating on Chinese social media, where users communicate by coining new 'English' phrases via calqued Chinese expressions, with the aim of implicitly critiquing social events through a ludic creative medium; see Li 2016; Lee & Li 2021: 559–62.) I also agree with Mair that Kongish resembles Singlish. I would add that the similarity rests in how they are enregistered into playful urban dialects in their respective locales, although Singlish may be seen as a predecessor of Kongish in terms of commodification, having generated a more mature industry around it (see Lee 2022a: Chs. 4–6).

However, Mair seems also to be conflating Kongish with HKE when he describes Kongish as being developed 'for decades' by Hong Kong users, who 'are apt to actually exchange whole sentences and even series of sentences in it'. This characterization points to the spoken vernacular, and therefore fits with HKE, but not Kongish, which is a new urban dialect *in writing*. It is crucial to recognize this re-semiotization from the spoken to the written and the way in which Kongish breaches the perceived boundary between the two. It is true that Kongish is intelligible only within its own exclusive circle of users – this is not necessarily co-extensive with the entire populace of English-language users in Hong Kong – based on 'a body of mutually agreed upon usages'. But it is important to highlight that these 'agreed upon usages' are in flux and not quite settled. At this point in time, Kongish is an experimental practice, in the sense that it is constantly inventive and not (yet) locked in as a code (and when it is one day consolidated into a code, it will then have lost its translanguaging potential). Which also means to say it is creative-in-flux, in that its combinations and permutations of English, Cantonese, and other semiotic resources are not exactly predictable or always iterable, although it does feature some recurrent salient features (see Section 3.2). Importantly, Kongish does not arise from neutral, everyday communications like HKE; rather, it is specifically designed to express a critical and cynical stance toward contemporary Hong Kong society. It is these features of Kongish that qualify it as a translanguaging praxis.

---

[28] https://languagelog.ldc.upenn.edu/nll/?p=20516 (emphasis added).

3.2 Case Examples

In what follows I will work through several examples from Kongish Daily, with a view to elucidating the salient translanguaging features that situate Kongish across the borders of languages and modalities in such a way as to render it xenophonic (see Section 1.3). My examples are selected from a larger base of web posts collected from Kongish Daily in the period August 2021– January 2022. They are selected to exemplify how Kongish users creatively manoeuvre linguistic and semiotic resources traditionally classified under discrete labels such as 'English', 'Cantonese', 'Mandarin', 'nonverbal signs', and so forth.

Figure 2 shows an announcement about two public forums on Hong Kong's English-language education, organized by the Centre for Language Education at the Hong Kong University of Science and Technology, where two of the Kongish Daily editors are based. Metalinguistically, the post conveys a characteristic irony by introducing – in Kongish, of course – an event on English conducted in Cantonese (as indicated in the postscript). The post's language is largely readable qua English, although it is replete with the following elements of 'textese':

a. idiosyncratic, eye-dialect spellings: *editer* instead of 'editor';
b. calques from Cantonese: *help help*: calqued from the Cantonese/Mandarin compound created by reduplicating the word for 'help';
c. contractions: *d*, standing for *di*, a Cantonese quantifier equivalent to 'some';
d. textisms: abbreviations or acronyms – *btw* for 'by the way', although this is not peculiar to Kongish; but CLS, standing for 'comment, like, share' (plain English meaning) and simultaneously invoking a colloquial term meaning 'insane' (ludic Cantonese meaning), is specifically Kongish (see my explanation below); and
e. transliterations from Cantonese: *ge* (possessive particle); *dou hai* ('are all/ both'); *yeah* ('things'), as well as coloured emojis at three points in the post.

The relative intelligibility of this passage qua English may suggest that the Cantonese segments represent instances of codeswitching. This, however, is not an adequate characterization of Kongish communications, where the putative identity of English as a matrix language is often destabilized by multiple Cantonese inflections on morphological, lexical, phonological, and syntactical levels. The construct that more sufficiently captures this type of discourse is translanguaging, with its emphasis not on the alternation between one code and another, but on the creative interplay of resources from different named languages.

KONGISH DAILY
Kongish Daily《港語日報》
30 August ·
Little editer is organising this event for teachers and anyone interested Come join us online or help help editer do d CLS ge yeah - comment, like or share this event to your friends
PS: both forums dou hai Cantonese btw!
Registration link:
https://cle.ust.hk/cle-public-forum-2021/

Figure 2 Help help editer do d CLS ge yeah.
Source: Kongish Daily, 30 August 2021.

The striking phrase in this example is *help help editer do d CLS ge yeah*, where the only English-proper words are 'help' and 'do', and where 'help', as indicated above, is reduplicated in a playful mimicry of Chinese syntax. The reflexive use of a professional title (*editer*) for self-reference is also marked in English but idiomatic in Chinese, although the idiosyncratic spelling here gives it a sense of the tongue-in-cheek. Another instance of aberrant spelling is the word *yeah*, a generic term in Cantonese for 'thing' or 'stuff'; the spelling here is not accidental, but contingently invented to invoke the adverb 'yeah' in informal English. This whole phrase is therefore only prima facie English. Contrary to its orthography, the phrase is rather more sensible as Cantonese: *bong*^{1} *bong*^{1} *siu*^{2} *pin*^{1} *zou*^{6} *di*^{1} *CLS ge*^{3} *je*^{5} 幫幫小編做點 CLS 嘅嘢, a perfectly grammatical phrase meaning 'help the little editor [read: me] do some CLS stuff'. The apparently English phrase is thus *translational*, syntactically calqued as it is from Cantonese.

As indicated above, CLS is an acronym for 'comment (C), like (L), (and) share' (S) in relation to social media posts. Yet for the seasoned Kongish user, a surreptitious duplicity is built into this instance of textism, evoking the vulgar phrase *ci*^{1} *lan*^{2} *sin*^{3} 痴闌線, meaning 'insane', alternatively construable as *ci*^{1} *nan*^{2} *sin*^{3} 痴撚線 where the second character refers to the male reproductive organ in colloquial Cantonese. Hence, what appears to be an innocuous English abbreviation relating to social media interactions is simultaneously interpretable as a vulgar Cantonese utterance – though only for those 'in the know', namely speakers of street Cantonese (mainly youths) who also have a working knowledge of written English.

CLS is exemplary of Kongish, for it is not unambiguously identifiable as *either* English *or* Cantonese; it embodies both at a single stroke. More specifically, the textism is bivalent (Woolard 1998) in its simultaneous invocation of different meanings on contrasting registers and across two genealogically distant languages, masquerading its identity in the one *through* the other (and vice versa), much like a turnstile. This raises the question of whether Kongish should at all be considered a variety of English, or what sociolinguists would call an instance of World (or Asian or Postcolonial) Englishes. This is a crucial issue that cuts through all the examples that follow.

Textisms like CLS are central to the Kongish lexicon – not an institutionalized lexicon obviously, but one marked with creative contingencies. They speak to the digital vernacular literacy that Kongish stands for. In Figure 3, the translingual acronymized exclamation WTF DLLM expresses revolting shock with respect to the image of a burger whose meat filling resembles poop. While WTF ('what the f*ck') is readily comprehensible to readers familiar with texting in English, DLLM is exemplary of Kongish. Literally equivalent to 'f*ck your mother', DLLM cleverly condenses a taboo Cantonese expletive (diu^2 lei^5 lou^5 mou^5 屌你老母) into a sleek acronym that can be conveniently slipped into any written discourse to express a hostile stance toward a given proposition (in the present example, a photograph).

In a manner of speaking, DLLM affectively translates WTF, adding locutionary force to the latter while demonstrating that Kongish, too, has the capacity to vulgarize in a euphemistic and economical way like colloquial English. In this instance, Kongish embodies a deceptive translingual operation, an invented cipher camouflaging an offensive epithet behind the double veil of romanization and acronymization. Indeed, the compactness and visual symmetry of DLLM afford it a superficial aesthetic evocative of a brand or corporate name (think D&G or LV for instance), though its meaning is anything but. This mischievous tension between the appearance of a 'cool' form and the substance of a 'not-so-cool' meaning is symptomatic of metrolanguages (see Maher 2005).

There is still English here, of course: 'what a replica', pointing again to the poop-like meat in the burger. This is followed by two emoticons depicting a monkey covering its eyes, suggesting that the picture of the burger is unsightly. This creates an interesting cohesion with the hashtag below the line: #cannotonlymeseeit. *Cannot only me see it* calques the Cantonese phrase for '[I] mustn't be the only one seeing it [this]', meaning the picture in the post needs to be shared widely. The tension between the monkey icon covering its eyes and the call for other people to view the unsightly image attests to the intersemiotics between text and image which, I argue, is part of the discourse itself.

Kongish Daily《港語日報》 ✓
6 December at 00:53 · 🌐

WTF DLLM what a replica

#cannotonlymeseeit

Figure 3 WTF DLLM. **Source:** Kongish Daily, 6 December 2021.

Adding to this cryptic quality of Kongish is its distinctive use of numbers. Not any random number, but semantically loaded ones with negative connotations in Cantonese (but not in Mandarin and English), namely 7 and 9. Both numbers connote stupidity or silliness. There is also a latent sexual connotation to these numbers, as when they are used in the nouns *luk¹ cat¹* 碌柒 and *luk¹ gau¹* 碌鳩 (both meaning 'penis'), where the second character in each word represents (in the second case, through homophony) 'seven' and 'nine' respectively. The two numbers appear most often in the invented forms *exac7ly* and *sor9ly*, as seen in Kongish Daily's mission statement (cited in Section 1). These forms comprise *intersemiotic morphologies*, where numbers are insinuated into alphabetic strings to create a monstrous (read: non-linguistic) entity. They exemplify how Kongish ruptures the visuality (spelling) and aurality (pronunciation) of English from within the latter's reading matrix.

Hence, with Kongish a new *guerrilla orthography* emerges from below, one that not only acknowledges the idiosyncrasies commonly associated with creolized English, but unabashedly flags them as a badge of place-based identity. *Exac7ly*, for instance, mimics how 'exactly' is perceived to be pronounced by non-native speakers of English in Hong Kong: *exac-tsat-ly*. In translating the mispronunciation (back) into the morphology of the English 'exactly' by way a number connoting stupidity, Kongish performs a self-mocking stance toward its own ostensible inadequacies as a Postcolonial English. At the same time, by giving form – a quirky, aberrant one – to the 'mispronounced' word, Kongish releases it from the strictures of English, returning the *language* to its *languaging* state.

In Figure 4, the translingual-cum-intersemiotic *9on9* typifies contingent, one-off formulations in Kongish that may appear trivial or nonsensical, but are in fact extremely complex in their morphological constitution. *On9* is meant to transcribe the Cantonese word *ngong⁶ gau¹* 戇鳩, meaning 'stupid', slyly tapping into the proximate pronunciation of the English 'on' in substitution for *ngong* ('stupid'). The second character *gau* denotes a species of bird and is homophonous to the character denoting the number 9 in Cantonese. And as explained above, 9 is one of those numbers in Cantonese with a negative, even sexual, connotation. While *on9* may be understandable to a Cantonese speaker, it gains a different valence in conjunction with the accompanying image, which shows a model, by a Japanese sculptor, depicting two birds, one standing on top of the other. The novel formulation *9on9*, then, translates into 'bird-on-bird', where 'on' is an English preposition that implicitly slides into the Cantonese *ngong* to connote the sense of 'stupidity'. Such linguistic games built on slippages between English and Cantonese, as well as between words and numbers/symbols, illustrate the capacity of Kongish to signify ludically between but also beyond languages. It is therefore Xenophonic in that it alienates its source languages, and even language as such.

Even more bizarre is *100 LAUGH9 50* in Figure 5. This alludes to the Chinese idiom 五十步笑百步, literally, 'fifty steps laughing at a hundred steps', the functional equivalent of 'the pot calling the kettle black' in English. Here the

Figure 4 9on9. **Source:** Kongish Daily, 4 November 2021.

two numbers are reversed to fit with the specific context of the news story, where the aged mother (whose seniority is represented by the number 100) of the late renowned Hong Kong celebrity Anita Mui critiques her son (whose relatively younger age is represented by the number 50) for eyeing Anita Mui's fortune. The number 9 attached to LAUGH indicates an authorial stance expressing cynicism, hinting at the silliness of the events related in the story. Notwithstanding the key word 'laugh', the largely numeric constitution of *100 LAUGH9 50* is such that it is a stretch to call it 'English' at all.

Kongish Daily《港語日報》 ✔

4 December at 16:30 · 🌐

100 LAUGH9 50?

TOPICK.HKET.COM

【梅艷芳】梅啟明稱自己從沒虧待阿梅　梅媽罕斥長子：他財迷心竅！

Figure 5 100 LAUGH9 50. **Source:** Kongish Daily, 4 December 2021.

Yet it cannot be called 'Chinese' either, for it is not based on a Sinitic script, although it translationally riffs off a Chinese-language idiom. Once again, the Xenophonic quality of Kongish comes to the fore in its relation to but alienation of both the Anglophone and the Sinophone. Like *9on9* above, *100 LAUGH9 50* also illustrates how Kongish is a written medium rather than a spoken one like

HKE; these formulations attract their ludic sense primarily in the form of online postings or texted messages.

Emojis and other icons further enhance the multimodal and ludic dimension of Kongish, creating a discourse that is *semiotically overdetermined*. By 'overdetermined', I mean Kongish is capable of manoeuvring all kinds of available resources in meaning-making, often speaking to both English and Cantonese at the same time and giving rise to bivalent readings, as we have seen above. Kongish thus speaks to a 'principle of abundance' (Li 2018a: 25; Lee & Li 2020: 409) where redundancy and intersemioticity are built into the discourse itself.

In Figure 6, for instance, the phrase 'Fairtrade Tea Leaf' is followed by the icon of a leaf, purely ornamental in this case. By contrast, in the subsequent clause, the icon of a panda's face substitutes the proper noun 'Food Panda', a popular food delivery service in Hong Kong and elsewhere. The clause thus translates as 'We should care a bit [more] about the welfare of those drivers from Food Panda [company]'. This interpretation is elicited partly from the news story, which is about delivery workers from Food Panda protesting against an enforced cut in their commission, and partly from the reader's locale-based knowledge about the corporate icon of the company in question.

This last sentence is also worked through by three Cantonese grammatical words: *har* (diminutive for verbs), *d* (demonstrative, 'those') and *gei* (possessive particle, which also appears in the first clause); and following Chinese grammar, the word 'driver' is not inflected for plurality. Now if we return to Figure 2 for a moment, we see the same Cantonese possessive particle in the phrase *help help editer do d CLS ge yeah*. Yet in Figure 6, we see the same particle spelled as *gei* instead of *ge*. This difference points to the inconsistency of Kongish orthography, illustrating the contingency of its form and hence its non-codified status – at this point in time, at least. In fact, Kongish Daily editors are themselves aware of the trappings of codification and make a conscious attempt not to bind themselves to any one 'correct' spelling in their postings. Instead, they take up the forms used by Kongish participants (including themselves) and recycle them without regard to normative rules of usage.[29]

All of this impedes reading from the vantage point of English-proper, although the sentence makes perfect sense if processed syntactically in Cantonese. Since the Cantonese words are not full content words, one could argue that this is not an instance of codemixing. It is rather translanguaging, where English and Chinese operate not in alternation but in tandem, requiring

---

[29] I would like to thank Alfred Tsang, Nick Wong, and Pedro Lok for providing me with this insight.

When supporting M&S gei Fairtrade Tea Leaf 🍃
We should care har d 🐼 Driver gei welfare...

阿成：啲單有時好過份，做九龍灣區，
要由Megabox送到入西貢喎，點幫佢送呀？

THESTANDNEWS.COM

【Foodpanda 罷工】罷工拒接單　電腦系統將減下周更
份　復工送遞員：變相懲罰 | 立場報道 | 立場新聞

Figure 6 Supporting Food Panda drivers.
Source: Kongish Daily, 19 November 2021.

one to *read translationally* in Cantonese (and in this case we may add Mandarin to the matrix) through the surface-level manifestation of English.

As an aside, in my reading of the phrase 'gei welfare', there is a further possibility of invoking the Mandarin word *gei* 给, meaning 'to give', such that the phrase is simultaneously interpretable as 'to provide welfare [to Food Panda drivers]', which is of course relevant to the proposition of the sentence. Note that this latter reading is entirely subjective; it may not be within the contemplation of the author of this post at all. It is my personal reading based on the composition of my repertoire. I'm a fluent user of Mandarin and English with partial proficiency in Cantonese, and it is this particular repertoire that facilitates my interpretation of *gei* as simultaneously Cantonese and Mandarin, even if the Mandarin interpretation may not have been intended. We might then venture to advance the argument that emerging discourses like Kongish are not closed systems, even if they primarily attract followers with largely similar repertoires. With Kongish, one needs to keep an open mind as to the notion of 'meaning', for its discourse is – as it should be – sometimes susceptible to interpretation in more ways than one, depending on the reader's specific repertoire. There is therefore a certain fuzziness in Kongish (as opposed to HKE, which is relatively more codified) that imbues it with dynamic potential and renders its boundaries fluid.

I mentioned earlier that Kongish often needs to be read translationally. This translational nature is evidenced in the extensive use of Cantonese-into-English calques in Kongish, often rendering an entire utterance virtually impenetrable to non-local English-language users. In Figure 7, *light light dick ask* calques the Chinese *hing¹ hing¹ dik¹ man⁶* 輕輕的問 ('to ask cautiously') morpheme-by-morpheme. Notice how, again, *dick* is bivalent and duplicitous, masquerading as the English word 'dick' – the choice of spelling here is no doubt calculated to produce a ludic, risqué effect – while transliterating the Cantonese adverbial particle *dik*. And just like *help help* in our first example above, the segment *light light* comes from the reduplicated compound *hing hing* ('softly, gently') in Chinese. Moving on to the second part of the clause, 'black shop' is calqued from *haak1 dim3* 黑店, a colloquial term referring to unethical businesses that do not provide value for money. The second clause, literally 'has anyone bought anything from the same black shop . . . like us', is again translational. It couches a grammatically Cantonese interrogative in an apparently English form, starting with the question word *yau mo* ('is there any') and affixing the verb 'purchase' with *jor* (a perfective aspect marker in Cantonese: has/have [bought]). Note also that the *mo* in *yau mo* is sometimes spelled *mou*, again pointing to inconsistencies in spelling and, as a corollary, the uncodified nature of Kongish.

Coupling with calques from Cantonese are locale-specific references that abound in Kongish Daily. In Figure 8, the expression *Place-wine at Big Happy* is impossible to understand without mentally back-translating the phrase into Cantonese; and even then, one needs to be familiar with Hong Kong's vernacular foodscape to know what the clause means. 'Place-wine' comes from

Little editer want to light light dick ask har - yau mo others purchase jor the same black shop 賣飛佛到會 My Favourite.Party Food like us 😊

■黑店「賣飛佛到會 My favourite.PartyFood」收完客錢確認訂單後，送餐當日打比個客話野食送唔到黎，仲要電話鬧個客 👍 🤬 😡

事源有朋友係 23/12 經 whatsapp 同「賣飛佛」到會訂餐，比曬全數確認訂單後，安排 27/12 5-6:15pm 送餐。

到 27/12 當日，朋友係下午 3 點已經 whatsapp 客服作溫馨提示 🔔 🔕，一直冇回覆 ❌。

朋友於是係下午 5 點打電話比公司再次確認 📞。公司比左送餐司機嘅電話叫朋友自己聯繫，朋友打去比司機點知個司機話唔係佢負責！😡

由 5pm-6pm，朋友一直透過 whatsapp 同電話聯絡「賣飛佛到會」，一直得唔到預計送餐時間嘅答覆，然後到 6:15pm，「賣飛佛」竟然打比朋友話司機送錯左地址，所有食物已經比啲客食曬！ 💀 👻

朋友打比「賣飛佛」，得到嘅答覆係野食送錯左都冇辦法，只可以安排即時退番全數款項，電話入面仲要鬧番個客轉頭！

👍😮 41   5 comments 1 share

Figure 7 Light light dick ask. **Source:** Kongish Daily, 28 December 2021.

calquing the Cantonese word *baai2 zau2* 擺酒, meaning to organize a (wedding) banquet. 'Big Happy' points to the ubiquitous and affordable café restaurant Fairwood, whose Chinese name 大快活 translates literally into 'big-happy'. This interpretation is made possible with the visual aid of the image, which shows Fairwood's logo and name. The post relates a couple's miserly decision to hold their wedding banquet at the inexpensive restaurant,

Place-wine at Big Happy 😎😎
Must be a memorable experience!

Actchooly, Editer suggest all-you-can eat lunch buffet McDonalds. Guess each guest won't eat you more than $100. Laisee $500 at least earn $400. More importantly, male guests can have Pretty Jei Jei play Mr Fox Now What Time with you 🦊🦉

Figure 8 Place-wine at Big Happy. **Source:** Kongish Daily, 5 November 2021.

suggesting instead that they do it at McDonald's – the sarcasm cannot be missed.

The final line, although mostly in English, apart from *Jei Jei* (literally 'older sister'),[30] here referring to young female waitresses at McDonald's, contains a baffling reference to *Mr Fox, What Time*; or more idiomatically, *What Time Is It, Mr Fox*? This latter segment, again, requires a back-translation into Cantonese, which yields the name of a popular children's game in Hong Kong, wu^4 lei^2 sin^1 $saang^1$ gei^2 do^1 dim^2 狐狸先生幾多點. But to understand how and why the game

---

[30] Note here that the spelling of *Jei Jei*, where the /ei/ is to be pronounced /e/, is variable. The other possible spelling is *Je Je*. This orthographic instability again points to the non-codified nature of Kongish; see my previous discussion in relation to the variation between *ge* and *gei*.

is related to McDonald's, one needs to know that it is common practice in Hong Kong for parents to reserve a section of a McDonald's restaurant to organize birthday parties for their children; and that during such events, waitresses (the *Jei Jei*) in the fast-food restaurant will usually join in to play games with the children attending the party, and *What Time Is It, Mr Fox?* is a metonym for such games. Conceivably, most users of English outside of Hong Kong would miss out on this connection. Yet part of the ludicity – not *lucidity* – of Kongish Daily's discourse stems from the trial-and-error guess-work sometimes involved in grasping the signified. This points to the fact that not all users of the English language, even those who are native to Hong Kong, would have the same ingredients in their repertoire (linguistic, semiotic, and cultural). This illustrates how Kongish can be xenophonic in its encryption of discourse in translational place-based idioms, whose signification is often not immediately obvious and must be traced, through either enquiring native informants or research into local practices.

Kongish discourse is highly reflexive and often engages in critical metalinguistic work in positioning itself vis-à-vis the English-language establishment. Figure 9 shows a post with an accompanying image of a bilingual sign in a street eatery. The English line, which reads 'Rice with two choices of sides [side dishes]', is already a fairly adequate translation of its Chinese counterpart. The post invites participants to contribute translations with the line *Yau mo highhand can suggest any?* – literally 'are there experts who can suggest any [translation]?', where *yau mo* is a Cantonese question word ('is/are there') and *high-hand* is a calque of the Chinese word *gou1 sau2* 高手, meaning accomplished persons. What is elicited here, of course, are not alternative English translations, but translations in Kongish.

The Kongish Daily editors give it a first go ('me first'): *Double Sung Rice*, where *sung* transliterates the Cantonese餸 for 'dish', while perhaps also calling out to the past tense of the verb 'sing' in English, or even 'song'. Here again, I must emphasize 'perhaps', because this latter interpretation is mine, and therefore entirely subjective and even slightly far-fetched; it may well be that this was not at all in the contemplation of the editors when penning the post. Yet as noted earlier, this also reflects the experimental, in-flux dimension of Kongish discourse, which thrives on a certain ambiguity as to the precise meaning of its formulations. The tongue-in-cheek translation *Double Sung Rice* would not make any sense from the point of view of communication. And communication is, of course, beside the point here. Rather, by interposing a Kongish translation on a pre-existing and perfectly intelligible bilingual sign, Kongish Daily makes a language ideological move here, implicitly construing Kongish as a viable and autonomous medium alongside English

Figure 9 Double Sung Rice.
Source: Kongish Daily, 9 January 2022.

(and also Cantonese for that matter). In so doing, the call-to-translation in the post affords Kongish an indexical value where its 'brokenness' in relation to English is not a source of stigma, but a *resource* for creative resistance against the taken-for-granted hegemony of English in Hong Kong's linguascape.

3.3 From Translanguaging to Commodification

Based on the preceding examples from Kongish Daily, we can see that Kongish as an evolving mode of communication is distinct, in terms of both form and ethos, from English in general and HKE in particular. But one should avoid listing the linguistic features of Kongish as if they were discrete (though, admittedly, I did that at two instances myself in relation to Figures 1 and 2, but that is with reference to specific posts on Kongish Daily, not to Kongish as an urban dialect). For to do so would be tantamount to recognizing the codified nature of Kongish, and that would be a misleading line to take. Kongish is rather an ever-evolving repertoire, not a fixated code like HKE offering itself up to lexicographers, and therefore one should instead refer to its propensities as well as to the discourse it constitutes. To put it tentatively and non-exhaustively, Kongish discourse entails the following:

a. a full range of linguistic performances, orchestrating not only recognizable features from English and Cantonese (and to a lesser extent, Mandarin), but also creative permutations and combinations of these features to generate new coinage 'on the whim';
b. the use of different written scripts, stylized signs and symbols (emoji icons and culturally loaded numbers), embedded images and videos as well as other visual devices (colours and typography), all converging on a single reading unit (a Facebook post) at once to make meaning; and
c. a playful subversiveness in the form of witty parodies of established linguistic forms and satirical commentaries on arising social events, where a critical and cynical stance is often camouflaged under the façade of humorous formulations.

In the terms developed in this study, Kongish Daily represents a virtual translanguaging space on social media where Hong Kong netizens come together to form a 'light' community of practice. A 'light' community is one comprising '*focused but diverse occasioned coagulations* of people . . . [who] converge or coagulate around a shared focus – an object, a shared interest, another person, an event' (Blommaert & Varis 2015: 54; original emphasis). In the case at hand, the shared object or interest is of course Kongish. As a community of practice, Kongish Daily is 'light', as are most communities formed around any nexus of interest on social media. Apart from the three editors managing the page and authoring the posts, the participants of Kongish Daily can come and go, reading and responding to the editors' posts (or not) at their own will. And apart from being virtual and 'light', Kongish Daily is, of course, à la Benedict Anderson (1983), also an imagined community, one that loosely coagulates around and contributes toward shaping the imagined urban dialect of Kongish.

Importantly, Kongish Daily does not impose rules of communication on its participants, especially on what kind of language to use or not to use, thus allowing features of Kongish to be 'crowdsourced', as it were, from the bottom up rather than applied from the top down. This aligns with Kongish Daily's empirical mission, which is to serve as a platform for observing as well as improvising momentary performances in Kongish giving voice to netizens. There is, therefore, a double hermeneutic (Smith & Osborn 2008) here, where the founders of Kongish Daily seek to make sense of how their fellow Hong Kong netizens make sense of their society through the medium of an imagined urban dialect (see Li et al. 2020: 314–15).

In creating a niche virtual space around an English-Cantonese vernacular, Kongish Daily also represents a form of commodification, in that it participates in the articulation of a translingual and multimodal register for public consumption on social media. Using the terms explained in Section 2, the rise of Kongish in recent years constitutes a symptom that the use of English in Hong Kong – retaining the somewhat problematic term 'English' for convenience now – has reached a $(N+1)+1$-th indexical order (Silverstein 2003), or a third order of indexicality (Johnstone 2009). This is the juncture where multilingual persons in Hong Kong are able to proactively appropriate the egalitarian ethos and grassroots values indexed by Kongish to engage in self-reflexive performances of cultural identities, often with a ludic stance that belies critical attitudes toward normative values. Like Singlish, Kongish as it is rolled out in Kongish Daily becomes an 'imprimatur of authenticity' (Wee 2018: 134), an expression of a particular kind of social persona (Heller 2010: 103), one firmly rooted in Hong Kong. Hence, to be capable of participating in Kongish Daily communications is to obtain a virtual identity membership exclusive to the 'insiders'.

Yet there is another form in which Kongish is commodified: it is also commoditized in tangible products in the marketplace. The evidence is available on the webpage of Kongish Daily itself, where there is an image under the label 'Shop'. Clicking the image brings up a pop-up advertisement window with the tagline:

KONGISH

Tee on sale. Made in Hong Kong (Tsuen Wan)

Kongish 'tee' refers to Kongish T-shirts, which aligns us directly with the parallel phenomena of Pittsburghese T-shirts (Johnstone 2009), Welsh T-shirts (Coupland 2012: 17–20), and Singlish T-shirts (Lee 2022a: 199–209). On the right panel of the advertisement, we are told – aptly, in Kongish:

KONGISH TEE now on sale!
- 100% made in HK (Tsuen Wan)
- Adult / Child size dou have

Very worth deal ar!
***Order page: https://thelimelights.co/collections/kongish
***Goodest photographer: donut photography

On the left panel are a series of photographs, taken by the '*goodest* photographer', showing models wearing T-shirts printed with the word Sor9ly, the iconic Kongish word for 'sorry'. The peculiar lexicogrammar of this advertisement – *dou have*; *very worth deal ar*; *goodest*; *sor9ly* – is by now familiar to us. What is interesting here is the collaboration between the social media platform Kongish Daily and a business entity in the promotion of Kongish-based merchandise. Apparently, the editors of Kongish Daily were approached by Hong Kong-based T-shirt manufacturers to provide the language and design ideas for creative cultural products. This is the point where Kongish becomes fetishized as part of the linguistic business of marketing (Kelly-Holmes 2020).

4 Commoditizing Kongish: The Linguistic Business of Marketing

> *Marketing is in fact an intensely linguistic business.*
> – Helen Kelly-Holmes, 'The linguistic business of marketing'

4.1 Gweilo: Kongish and Entrepreneurship

I want to start with one of the most enigmatic words in the colloquial lexicon of Hong Kong: *gweilo*. Comprising the Cantonese morphemes *gwai* (ghost, devil) and *lou* (man, bloke, or vulgar person), and settled into the romanized form *gweilo*, the word today refers generally to persons of Caucasian descent (in the colonial days, primarily the British). On the face of the etymology, it is a term of insult, and indeed many a foreigner in Hong Kong still takes offence on being referred to as, literally, a 'ghost-man'. This is evidenced in a 2018 lawsuit where a British engineer sued his employer for addressing him as *gweilo* in the course of his employment in Hong Kong, which, to the plaintiff, amounted to discrimination. The claim was dismissed in 2022 by a Hong Kong court, which opined that the term does not necessarily indicate racist intentions.[31]

Irrespective of the court verdict, the jury is still out as to whether *gweilo* is a racist epithet.[32] The sinologist Victor Mair contends that the term is indeed discriminatory, maintaining that it is 'overtly, inherently, intentionally racist':

---

[31] https://www.scmp.com/news/hong-kong/law-and-crime/article/3166759/cantonese-slang-gweilo-not-racist-judge-rules.

[32] See, for instance, two *SCMP* articles on this subject, 'Is the term "gweilo" racist slang?' by Alex Lo (SCMP, 10 Nov 2021) and 'Is "gweilo" really a racist word? Hong Kong just can't decide' by Yonden Lhatoo (SCMP, 8 Sep 2018).

It stigmatizes an entire race as inferior beings. If any white person tells you that it is not racist, they are being self-effacing/deprecating or ironic . . . If a Chinese person says that it is a neutral or positive appellation for a Caucasian, they are either being disingenuous or evidently do not know the meanings of the constituent morphemes.[33]

For our purposes, the debate around *gweilo* foregrounds its valence as an intercultural nexus. The word is quintessentially Hong Kong, invoking as it does the historical tensions between the local Chinese and their British rulers during the territory's 150-year history as a crown colony. It is against the historical baggage and ethnic connotation of *gweilo* that its recent commodification as a brand name in Hong Kong becomes a meaningful phenomenon for discussion.

Enter *Gweilo*, a successful craft beer company founded in 2014 by three British expatriates in Hong Kong.[34] Following Mair's understanding (cited earlier), this use of *gweilo* for self-reference could evince a self-effacing, ironic stance on the part of the founders. Apparently this is not the case with the company's co-founder Ian Jebbitt, for whom *gweilo* has shed much of the burden of its negative connotations, having 'done a full U-turn from having negative connotations 30 years ago, to not having those connotations now'.[35] In the event, the real irony lies not in a Briton's use of *gweilo* for playful self-reference, but in the fact that it was Jebbitt who had to convince local authorities in Hong Kong on its feasibility as a trademark:

> [T]he trademark registry is quite conservative . . . and it did initially reject it on the basis of it being derogatory, but I spent three months putting together a legal submission showing how the word is not being used in this racially deprecating manner . . . and it was accepted.[36]

I want to argue that this reflexive naming strategy represents the capacity of language users (not necessarily the local Hong Kongers) to move beyond using language to index ethnic or class relations, to performing locale-specific dynamics through language. The originally derogatory term *gweilo*, in effect, has become commodified into an entrepreneurial concept in virtue of its becoming a trademark. More specifically, the stereotyped persona associated with the term (Caucasians) in the cultural imaginary of local Hong Kong people is

---

[33] This extract is taken from Victor Mair's blog piece, '"Gweilo" as a racially charged term', in his *Language Log* (10 September 2018), https://languagelog.ldc.upenn.edu/nll/?p=39947.

[34] https://gweilobeer.com/.

[35] Quoted in https://www.scmp.com/lifestyle/food-drink/article/2113382/gweilo-beer-open-hong-kongs-biggest-craft-brewery-keep-demand.

[36] Ibid.

commoditized in the form of saleable artefacts. It is important to note, therefore, that the term *gweilo* itself does not necessarily encapsulate translanguaging (see Section 2) and hence is not always an instance of Kongish. In itself in romanized form, it is simply HKE; when uttered in Cantonese in ordinary conversations to refer to foreign persons, it is just that – a Cantonese epithet. It is only when the term is used with a creative and/or critical intent that *gweilo* qualifies as a Kongish word and instantiates translanguaging.

In the case at hand, not only is *gweilo* commodified as the name of the brand and company but it is also emplaced on beer cans, pint glasses, and the like. There is a crucial process of remediation here, turning a most ordinary Cantonese word (or HKE word when romanized) into an emplaced sign on a material item that calls attention to its own markedness in a commodity context. It is this remediating process and the markedness it produces that give the term a translanguaging edge.

Figure 10 shows a pint glass sold by Gweilo. On its surface is printed the brand name (gwei.lo), followed by a block of text resembling a lexical entry in a dictionary. The text first gives us the Chinese characters for the word *gweilo*, followed by its pronunciation in IPA (International Phonetic Alphabet) transcription. It then introduces the word as a noun, with the plural form *gweilos*. As per a conventional dictionary entry, the word is first given a literal gloss as the Cantonese term for 'ghost chap'. This is linguistically sound. Then the text proceeds with an ostensibly 'historical' gloss of *gweilo* as 'a Cantonese slang term used to describe barbarian hedonistic invaders of Canton in the 16th century'. Now this putative definition is intended to be humorously dubious, because according to historical facts, in the sixteenth century, foreigners had not yet penetrated China, much less invaded Canton. The word 'hedonistic' also gives us a clue that this is a playful definition, one that coheres with the underlying beer theme. The text then offers a modern usage of the term as describing foreigners 'in the first and third person'. This latter reference to the use of *gweilo* for self-address ('first person') is a reflexive move pointing to the company's own strategy of using an apparently derogatory term to refer to themselves (recall that the company's founders are all British). Finally, the 'dictionary entry' comes to its main point, defining *gweilo* as a registered trademark: 'Exceptional craft beer brewed in Hong Kong with talent, expertise and above all, modesty'. It even offers a phrase in the style of a sample sentence we see in the *OED* or *Merriam Webster*: 'A chilled and full-bodied gweilo can be surprisingly sophisticated'.[37]

---

[37] In another version of the same text on a gin bottle (see Figure 11), the 'sample sentence' is: 'Cool and well-balanced, a gweilo is the epitome of refinement and good taste'.

Figure 10 Gweilo beer. **Source:** https://gweilobeer.com/.

This piece of emplaced text on the pint glass, also printed on other Gweilo products such as T-shirts, gin bottles, and bottle coolers (Figure 11), is intriguing in how it uses a recognizable template of a quasi-lexicographical entry to enframe its brand name in a positive light, thus decontextualizing the Cantonese term from its derogatory usage and recontextualizing it along the trajectory of ludic marketing. It demonstrates a resourcefulness on the part of Hong Kong-based

Figure 11 Gweilo merchandise printed with 'definition' of *gweilo*. From left to right: T-shirt, gin bottle, and bottle cooler sleeves.

Source: https://gweilobeer.com/.

entrepreneurs in commoditizing urban dialects in marketing communications. This again evidences that Kongish, in the form of romanized Cantonese here, has entered what we have explained as the third indexical order (see Section 2), where a linguistic feature, in this case the culturally loaded and still-controversial term *gweilo*, is re-semiotized from the vernacular Cantonese register into an entrepreneurial context where it becomes of a piece of intellectual property – the trademark Gweilo.

4.2 The Fok Hing Gin Controversy

Gweilo recalls another controversial trademark, also a brand of alcoholic beverage: Fok Hing Gin (Figure 12). Founded in 2017, Fok Hing Gin, based in Hong Kong and also registered in the UK, caused a controversy in 2021 when the UK's alcoholic drinks industry watchdog Portman Group received a complaint that the brand name was sexually offensive. The name Fok Hing, literally 'fortune [and] prosperity' is based on a certain Fuk Hing Lane in Hong Kong's famous neighbourhood Causeway Bay. It is therefore a place-based appellation – or so it could be argued. But the UK watchdog's Independent Complaints Panel (ICP) determined that the company's name bears the obvious intention 'to shock and offend those who find swearing undesirable and unacceptable'.[38] The company was also reported to have used punned phrases like 'fok off' and 'fokthehaters' in their marketing communications.[39] It was eventually held that Fok Hing Gin was in breach of Clause 3.3 of the Code of Practice on the Naming, Packaging and Promotion of Alcoholic Drinks, which states: 'A drink's name, its packaging and any promotional material or activity should not cause serious or widespread offence.[40]

In its defence, Fok Hing Gin submitted that the ICP 'had taken an overly cautious position and that the phonetic expression of the phrase "Fok" was more likely understood as the word "feck" would be, which was defined as "medium strength" language'. And to be fair, the company had earlier already altered the original *Fuk Hing* in romanized Cantonese to *Fok Hing* to avoid offending Western-language sensibilities – using *Fuk* would conceivably cause even greater problems. Apparently, this tactical respelling of *Fuk* as *Fok* didn't do the trick. In response to the ICP's decision, the company did not propose to change its appellation, but nevertheless agreed to take positive actions to mitigate its offensiveness. Specifically, the company would 'redesign the back label of the product to include a graphic representation of "Fuk Hing Lane" and would also include a descriptive narrative of the brand story to provide context

---

[38] For a full report of the decision, see https://www.portmangroup.org.uk/fok-hing-gin/.
[39] Ibid.   [40] Ibid.

Figure 12 Fok Hing Gin. **Source:** https://fokhinggin.com.

for consumers regarding the name and heritage of the product'. It would also indicate how the name should be properly pronounced by way of printing the transliteration of the Chinese term using the Cantonese romanization system on the back label of its UK products.[41]

Notwithstanding the legal dimension of the issue, I am more interested in the company's motivation to commodify a street name in Cantonese, via romanization, into a potentially sensitive brand name for marketing its product to an anglophone clientele, both in Hong Kong and in the UK. Like the owners of Gweilo, the proprietors of Fok Hing Gin are evidently aware of the implication

---

[41] https://www.portmangroup.org.uk/fok-hing-gin/.

of their brand name from the outset, as seen from how they introduce their brand on their website:

> Our name sounds like a popular western profanity, you say? Whilst that is a remarkable coincidence, we are actually named after a street in our Hong Kong hometown; a name the locals have long since stopped guffawing at. But many visitors to our fine city still see the funny side and we are OK with that. We laugh at ourselves, so why not let visitors in on it? So happy are we, in fact, that we adopted the street name for our gin.[42]

The casual tone of this text and the statement 'We laugh at ourselves, so why not let visitors in on it?' points to a ludic, self-reflexive appropriation of the vernacular language and, as with the Gweilo case, evidences that Kongish operates on the third indexical order. This is because only on this order can romanized Cantonese be self-consciously enregistered by persons for identity work – and further, be transformed into a commoditization strategy. In their ICP submission, the company conceded that their choice of the appellation 'could be prompted by humour and curiosity at the brand name', and that 'some aspects of its marketing used novelty and humour', while stressing that the choice of the name was to expose its consumers to Hong Kong's cultural heritage behind it.[43] This shows that playfulness has always already been embedded in the company's branding and marketing strategy. And according to Johnstone et al. (2006: 83), one symptom of an urban dialect's third-order indexicality is the propensity of its speakers to 'use regional forms drawn from highly codified lists to perform local identity, often in ironic, semiserious ways'. This ironic, semi-serious stance, a naughtiness if you like, is demonstrated by Fok Hing Gin in how it responded to the controversy around their brand in a post on their Facebook page dated 12 November 2021 (Figure 13).

This post represents a very different response to the controversy on the part of Fok Hing Gin, showing the company's pushback against the complaint associated with its brand name. Whereas the company's submission to the ICP inquiry is generally positive in tone, their Facebook post in Figure 13 is decidedly ludic. The signatory of the post is a certain 'Holly Fok', which riffs off the expletive 'holy f**k' and is almost certainly not the real name of the person authoring the post. In a tongue-in-cheek manner, the post responds sarcastically to 'the Karen' (note the definite article here), supposedly the name of the person who first lodged the complaint to the UK watchdog. The post first recapitulates on the geographical genesis of the name Fok Hing, and asks the complainant not to 'get your Primark g-strings twisted' upon seeing the brand name. It promises to update the reverse label of their bottles to provide a richer cultural background

---

[42] https://fokhinggin.com/.   [43] https://www.portmangroup.org.uk/fok-hing-gin/#_ftn1.

To the Karen who got offended by our name...

We're genuinely sorry.

...that you haven't had the experience of different cultures and their unique diversities. We'd be delighted to show you around Hong Kong one day (if you ever make it past its borders!)

As you know, our gin pays special homage to
FUK HING LANE in Causeway Bay,
and not quite what you think it sounds like.

So no need to get your Primark g-strings twisted, we'll make sure to update our back label with a more descriptive narrative of our brand story. We're almost out of labels anyways from our award-winning sell-out gin!

PS Thank you, you've helped us go viral and generated more press and traffic we could ever imagine – more effective than a PR agency! Might we suggest a new hobby?

Sincerely,
Holly Fok

Figure 13 Fok Hing Gin's response to a complaint about its controversial name. **Source:** https://www.facebook.com/fokhinggin/photos/pb.100064160041680.-2207520000../889690325001830/.

to the name – the same action promised in the company's submission to the ICP – but adds: 'We're almost out of labels anyways from our award-winning sell-out gins!' Of course, the company has not really run out of labels; this latter statement is a playful insinuation that despite – or because of – their name, they have proved to be a bestseller. The post then turns the tables around to 'thank' the complainant for helping them attract more media coverage, and concludes, with a sarcasm that cannot be missed, that 'the Karen' should consider media public relations as a new vocation.

4.3 Fetishizing Kongish

The Gweilo and Fok Hing Gin episodes are more recent sagas around contentious Kongish-based appellations across languages and cultures.[44] But it is precisely the controversial nature of such locale-specific words that is worth investigating in the context of linguistic commodification. This takes us to what Kelly-Holmes (2020) calls the 'linguistic business of marketing' with respect to Hong Kong's commodity situation (see Section 2).

A key aspect of the linguistic business of marketing is visual consumption, which is 'a key attribute of an experience economy organized around attention' (Schroeder 2006: 6). Hence, for example, the terms *gweilo* and *fok hing* call attention to themselves by way of their visible emplacement on alcohol-related products. The centrality of visuality is illustrated in the quasi-dictionary template adopted by Gweilo and its replication across a series of products (Figures 10 and 11). It is also evident in how Fok Hing Gin puts out merchandise such as tote bags and cocktail-shaker sets imprinted with its brand name, and also in its intention to include a graphic representation of Fuk Hing Lane on the back label of its bottles to foreground the place-based origin of its brand name. These examples exemplify the fetishization of language for commercial purposes (Kelly-Holmes 2014, 2020). Here, fetishization refers to the idea of language being re-semiotized into a visual signifier, which local entrepreneurs can extrapolate into creative marketing resources by tapping into entrained notions of 'authentic cultural membership' (Coupland 2003: 417) in Hong Kong.

And one should add that in the above two cases, it is not just the visuality, but also the aurality of the Kongish epithets that matters, and this is most evident in the Fok Hing Gin controversy discussed earlier, with its phonetic pun on the English expletive. In more technical terms, we might say that on the third order of indexicality, Kongish is not only used reflexively as a critical medium to articulate a community of practice, as in Kongish Daily (Section 3); its visual-aural forms are also proactively commoditized by local entrepreneurs, hence turning the urban dialect into a resource not just for identity work (which operates on the second order of indexicality), but as a marketing concept. And this is where Kongish departs from HKE: whereas HKE can be said to be a medium of communication among Hong Kong persons, Kongish extends beyond the instrumentality of everyday talk, always carrying with it a ludic self-reflexivity that HKE arguably does not possess.

---

[44] For other examples, see https://www.augustman.com/sg/food-drink/drinks/the-fuss-about-fok-hing-gin-and-timah-whiskey-and-other-offensive-spirits/.

The fetishization of urban dialects like Kongish for marketing should also be understood as dovetailing with global tourism discourses, of which text-based collectibles are a part. We have already seen, for instance, that apart from their beer products, companies like Gweilo and Fok Hing Gin also design affiliate merchandise imprinted with their brand names. Products such as these instantiate the social, economic, and symbolic orders of mobility (Jaworski & Thurlow 2010), a key aspect of the experience economy. In this regard, the commoditization of Kongish represents the remediation of vernacular resources into diacritics of 'commodity registers' (Agha 2011). Pietikäinen et al. (2016: 108) argue that peripheral languages – and Kongish must be considered peripheral vis-à-vis English – can 'cast a semiotically rich aura of "luxury" upon otherwise mundane products'. It is a commonplace that global languages like English or French are mobilized to index cosmopolitanism and modernity in respect of products or businesses. But with the rise of tourism in non-Western or minority regions, local urban dialects like Kongish too are fetishized for their value-adding potential as visual-aural signifiers of authenticity. This is to satisfy the voyeuristic curiosities of what Peterson and Kern (1996) call cultural omnivores (see Theng & Lee 2022).[45]

In other words, Kongish has attracted what sociolinguists call *covert prestige* (Trudgill 1972). It is not simply a medium of communication, which HKE arguably is. Rather, by virtue of its impenetrability by non-local persons, Kongish has come to index a sort of *subaltern classiness* signalling solidarity among persons-in-the-culture. It is this new value that makes it possible for Kongish to be fetishized as a commodity on its own terms. Put simply, when one buys a T-shirt imprinted with a Kongish epithet, it is the epithet that provides value to the user, not the T-shirt: the tangible item of transaction (the T-shirt) is in fact only a medium for the actual commodity, namely the urban dialect; or more specifically, the covert prestige endowed by that dialect.

This fetishization of Kongish has led to the emergence of text-based collectibles. We have already seen some examples with fabricated definitions of the term *gweilo*, such as the pint glass and bottle cooler sleeve (Figures 10 and 11). Now let us look at another example. Figure 14 shows an artefact I bought from a shop in Hong Kong's Wan Chai neighbourhood specializing in paraphernalia for the Chinese New Year celebrations. It is one in a series of eight red envelopes called *laisee* in Cantonese. The term refers to envelopes used for

---

[45] Where, cultural omnivores, according to Brown-Saracino (2009: 192, cited in Wee 2018: 133), are persons who embody 'an ethos that values a sort of cultural democracy that embraces a familiarity with low-, middle-, and highbrow cultural objects alike – that celebrates the idiosyncratic character of people and place'. This ethos manifests in an appreciation or even preference for underdog languages and cultures.

Figure 14 'Fat like a pig head' envelope. Author's photo.

the giving of petty cash symbolizing the exchange of blessings during the Chinese New Year.

At first blush, the English text appears shocking: *Fat Like a Pig Head*. In small print on the top right-hand corner are the words 'wish you', so prima facie this expression can be interpreted as a wish for someone to become 'fat like a pig head'. This surely sounds like an insulting remark and would be scandalous in a Chinese New Year context, where the usual *laisee* would feature auspicious sayings in formulaic, typically four-character Chinese expressions. The twist to this expression is that it is only *apparently* English, but is in fact a partial calque of a four-character phrase in Cantonese: *faat³ gwo³ zyu¹ tau⁴* 發過豬頭. Literally 'to make a fortune larger than a pig head', the expression conveys good wishes for the receiver of the red envelope to become wealthier in the new year. The English calque 'fat like a pig head' instantiates Kongish, precisely because it makes no sense, or rather misleads one to the wrong sense, when interpreted in English. The four words would be completely baffling for non-local persons, including Chinese-language users who are unfamiliar with idiomatic Cantonese – myself included, at least initially. It is the slippage between the literal negative meaning of the English calque and the actual positive connotation of the original Cantonese expression that generates humour; and it is within this slippage between English and Cantonese that translanguaging manifests in the form of Kongish.

4.4 Kongish T-shirts and Other Merchandise

By far the most common Kongish-based products are T-shirts and other apparels. Kongish T-shirts and other related collectibles connect with a larger constellation of artefacts produced globally across different locales. They are on the same order of things as Johnstone's (2009) Pittsburghese shirts printed with words from Pittsburgh's urban dialect. As explained in Section 2, it is when an urban dialect reaches third-order indexicality that it can enter its 'commodity phase' and become commoditized, for instance, into Pittsburghese shirts. For Johnstone (2009: 159), Pittsburghese shirts 'are not simply evidence of dialect awareness'; they are 'part of a process leading to the creation and focusing of the idea that there is a Pittsburgh dialect in the first place', and tend to emanate 'a youthful sense of urban hipness' (Johnstone 2010: 399). Pittsburghese shirts, among other kinds of sellable items marked with Pittsburghese such as coffee mugs and postcards, are therefore a window on how Pittsburghers, ex-Pittsburghers, as well as visitors from outside of Pittsburgh come to 'share ideas about what Pittsburgh speech consists of and what it means' (Johnstone 2009: 159).

Similar developments have been attested elsewhere, as in Welsh-language T-shirts, which Coupland (2012: 17) describes as representing a bottom-up, 'laconic metacultural celebration' of Welshness. Laconic, because the meanings of the texts on these T-shirts are often ludic and esoteric, evincing 'a noninsistent orientation and a laidback tolerance of incomplete meaning making' (p. 19). And metacultural, because these T-shirts thematize 'language-in-Wales' by means of a stylized Welsh – Welsh blended with English, Italian, and Spanish to create a 'polylingual bricolage' (p. 18) – as well as oblique references to 'deeply-coded Welsh historical and cultural phenomena and events' (p. 20). And finally, celebratory, because these T-shirts flag the centrality of Welsh to the identity of their wearers as hailing from Wales as opposed to England.

Elsewhere (Lee 2022a: 192–209), I noted the rise of similar T-shirts, among a wider range of memorabilia, featuring Singlish epithets comprising Hokkien (the dominant Chinese dialect in Singapore), colloquial Malay, English, and Mandarin Chinese. I pointed out that '[t]he potential mobility of vernacular T-shirts connects with their rhetorical and social function to project an egalitarian ethos with a dose of political incorrectness and playful resistance. In this regard, the heteroglossic and multimodal constitution of the language on these T-shirts affords them a sense of naughtiness and cynicism' (Lee 2022a: 208).

The same observations apply to Kongish T-shirts and other memorabilia, which have emerged more recently than analogous products in Pittsburghese, Welsh, and Singlish. The Hong Kong company *Goods of Desire*, better known in its quirky acronym G.O.D., is a pioneer in this niche industry. G.O.D. products are all designed around a place-based nostalgic theme. This is proclaimed on the company's webpage, which states that their designs 'are inspired by the vibrant culture of this energetic city where east meets west, and age-old traditions meet cutting-edge technology. With humour and creativity, we turn everyday subjects into truly extraordinary objects'.[46] The reference to creativity and humour recalls our characterization of the semi-serious stance of third-order indexicals (see Table 1) and the ludification of culture as expressed through translanguaging.

Thus, many of G.O.D.'s products are replete with humorous Cantonese-based epithets in Kongish, and the humour often comes from the translanguaging spaces it creates on its commodities. The brand name G.O.D. itself is a multilayered pun. Its full form is Goods of Desire; its abbreviation, of course, invokes the word 'God'; but, when read out letter-by-letter in Cantonese, it sounds like the Cantonese phrase zyu^6 hou^2 di^1 住好啲, sometimes written as

---

[46] https://god.com.hk/pages/about-us.

住好D, which means 'to live better'. Not all of G.O.D.'s products are text-based, but it carries a product line called 'Graphics T-shirts series' that provides ample examples on how Kongish is commoditized in refreshingly mischievous ways.

Figure 15a shows a first set of examples. *9up* (top-left) is an example of culture jamming, defined as 'the practice of parodying advertisements and hijacking bill-boards in order to drastically alter their images' (Klein 2000: 280), and described as '[p]erhaps the most radical form of genre-based subversion of dominant narratives' (Baker 2019: 94). *9up* 'jams' the design and colour scheme of the soft drink company 7up's logo, inserting the G.O.D. logo in-between. And we should recall that 9 (together with 7) is a culturally loaded number in Cantonese connoting silliness. The *Sor9ly* T-shirt (top-right) works along the same logic (and we have already encountered the term *sor9ly* in Kongish Daily's mission statement), with the number 9 printed in red to highlight its prominence. *Momentalia* (bottom-left) creatively transliterates the Cantonese phrase *mou⁵ man⁶ tai⁴ laa¹* 冇問題啦 into a nonce-word. This nonce-word embeds the English word 'moment', but also evokes Latin-sounding words ending with the suffix *-alia*, denoting things relating to a particular area of activity or interest, such as 'kitchenalia', 'orientalia', 'marginalia', 'personalia', and the like. The epithet *Mont Mer à Mon* (bottom-right) is extremely clever in its evocation of French and reference to a mountain as depicted on the T-shirt. The uninformed reader might think this is the name of an actual mountain in France. The humour sets in when we come to the bottom line: 'What are you looking at?', which in an instant of bathos turns the elegant-sounding 'French' name into an aggressive Cantonese interrogative: *mong6 me1 aa3 mong6* 望咩呀望, roughly 'what the hell are you looking at?' As it turns out, *Mont Mer à Mon* is a quasi-transliteration of the Cantonese interrogative, orthographically tweaked (even adding a diacritic to *à*) into a nonsense word cleverly couched as 'French'.

In Figure 15b, *Confuciusly* (top-left) is an invented word that invokes the English word 'confusingly'. It also morphologically inflects 'Confucius', the name of the most famous ancient Chinese philosopher and his school of thought, with the *-ly* suffix; this gives it a metalinguistic twist, as the nonce-word is itself *confusingly* spelled to the uninformed reader. *Sigh Gas* (top-right) calques the Cantonese term *saai¹ hei³* 嘥氣 literally, 'waste breath', which means to put effort into something in vain. Note that on top of the calque, the word 'sigh' transliterates *saai¹*: they sound similar in tone, though the Cantonese word has a prolonged vowel. And the second word *hei³* is given the literal translation 'gas' rather than 'breath', as the Cantonese word can also be used in the Chinese compound word for petrol gas, *hei³ jau⁴* 汽油. The two

Figure 15a Kongish-based apparels from G.O.D.

Figure 15b Kongish-based apparels from G.O.D.

Figure 15c Kongish-based apparels from G.O.D.

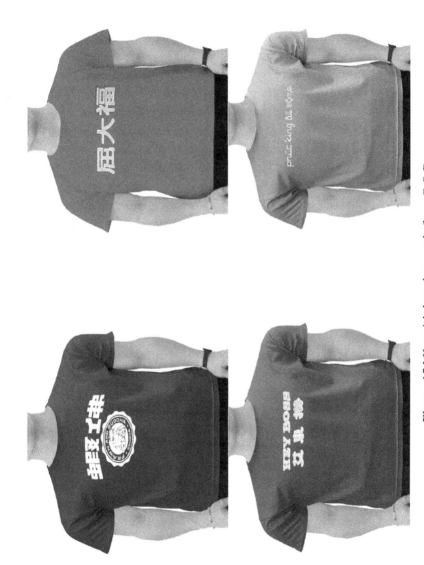

Figure 15d Kongish-based apparels from G.O.D.

images at the bottom exhibit the same phrase, 'delay no more', on a T-shirt and an undergarment. On the T-shirt (bottom-left), the phrase follows 'Stop climate change', so as an English expression, 'delay no more' would mean a call-to-action ('act now'). But in fact, this phrase is extremely cunning. As it turns out, *delay no more* is a syllable-by-syllable imitation of the sound of the Cantonese expletive *diu² lei⁵ lou⁵ mou⁵* 屌你老母 (literally, 'f**k your mother'): <u>de</u>=*diu*; <u>lay</u>=*lei*; <u>no</u>=*lou*; <u>more</u>=*mou*. And when the same phrase is emplaced on other apparels, in particular men's undergarments (bottom right), the sexual undertone in the Cantonese expletive gains a laconically corporeal sense. *Delay no more* is in fact one of those signature Kongish phrases invented by G.O.D. and is emplaced on several other products such as doormats and notebooks.

Figure 15c shows another set of T-shirt products where the epithets are bilingual in Kongish and Chinese, mostly with allusions to locale-specific idioms and cultural practices. The top-left image displays the term *Big Bamboo Motel*, which is completely opaque in English. It is only with reference to the Chinese lines above that it makes sense. The four characters at the top in small print reads: 'Room rental only'. This is a ubiquitous sign in cheap hotels located within high-rise buildings in Hong Kong to indicate that the hotel provides only accommodation without 'extra' (sexual) services. In the second line, the first two characters 大碌 are an adjective for describing thick and elongated things such as bamboo smoking pipes, and are a euphemism for 'penis'; the latter two characters 小築 literally mean 'small house', mimicking how hotel resorts on outlying islands style their names. Big Bamboo Motel is thus a quasi-translation of this second line in Chinese, where 'big bamboo' has a sexual innuendo with reference to the Chinese adjective it calques. And in the context of the top line, the whole Kongish phrase obliquely references how couples tend to book cheap hotels for their intimate moments. *The Force of Ten Thousand Buddhas* (top-right) is again a quasi-translation, this time of the Chinese phrase 萬佛朝中. As depicted in the cartoon figure on the T-shirt, the phrase refers to an ultimate kung fu style that evokes old-school Hong Kong martial arts movies. Like many of the other examples, this kind of 'English' does not make any sense to an English-language user without the sociocultural context surreptitiously embedded in the epithet.

The bottom-left image in Figure 15c that reads 小心 PK, literally 'be careful of PK', is not emplaced on a T-shirt but on a bathroom mat. I included this example here for two reasons. First, because the word PK, abbreviated from *puk1 gaai1* 仆街, is such a signature Hong Kong word, literally meaning 'to fall down on the street' but always used as a swear word. Second, the example illustrates the ludic self-reflexivity of Kongish as it is commoditized. In this case, the emplacement of the phrase 小心 PK on a floor carpet points to the danger of slipping in a way that re-semiotizes a vulgar word into an entertaining epithet – but again, only for those in the know. This demonstrates a high creativity in using resources from the vernacular and integrating them into multimodal artefacts. The last example on the bottom-right features the Cantonese phrase 你咪L嘈 which means 'shut up', where the letter 'L' is often used in Kongish as an abbreviated expletive.[47] On the T-shirt, the man figure with an angry look is holding a yellow bottle with the label *Lemoncello*; this is a made-up name mimicking *Limoncello*, an Italian lemon-based liquor brand distinguished by its yellow bottles. What makes the invented name *Lemoncello* Kongish is that it simultaneously plays on the appellation *Limoncello* and vaguely transliterates the Cantonese phrase meaning 'shut up', especially when read quickly: *lei^5 mai^5 (L) cou^4*.

My last set of examples in Figure 15d comprise texts that are not, on the face of it, even English. They play on masquerading one language beneath the other. Masquerading is a core technique in Kongish discourse; it teases the reader to read the one language through the other, and it is in the transient space between the two languages that contingent creativity, a key attribute of translanguaging, comes through. We have already seen this operating in many of the previous examples, but in those cases, it is normally an apparently English text camouflaging a Cantonese expression. The present set of examples turn this around to camouflage English beneath the surface level form of the Chinese script. As with the preceding examples, these also exemplify translanguaging, because even though most of them feature Chinese characters, they are incomprehensible without a knowledge of *both* Cantonese and English. And most importantly, there is always a playful twist to them.

In the top-left image in Figure 15d, we see the words 蝦佛, literally 'prawn-Buddha'. This literal translation is printed in the centre of the T-shirt as *Prawn and Buddha*, curved around a logo that features a prawn-headed creature sitting in a meditative position – like a Buddha. *Prawn and Buddha* obviously makes no sense in English. One must have recourse to the Cantonese pronunciation of the two Chinese characters: *haa^1 fat^6*, and relate this to the visuality of the logo, reminiscent of that of a company or school. It is at this moment that one realizes that the two Chinese characters are not really Chinese after all: they transliterate 'Harvard': <u>har</u>: *haa;* <u>vard</u>: *fat* (pronounced like 'fud' as in 'mud'). Thus, the name of a prestigious university has now been transposed into the ludicrous appellation *Prawn and Buddha* via creative transliteration. One should note that this interpretation is viable only with recourse to the logo, which provides a clue to the linguistic

---

The character represented by the letter 'L' is *lan^2* 撚, literally referring to the male sexual organ in Cantonese and is often used in colloquial speech as an intensifier.

riddle. This shows the multimodal dimension immanent in Kongish communications.

The next two images are designed using the same concept: the T-shirt on the top-right shows the characters 屈大福, which do not make up an understandable Chinese word; the last two characters, literally 'big' and 'bliss' respectively, seem to indicate that the 'word' has a positive connotation. It is only when these characters are romanized that it becomes clear that the reverse is true: wat^1 $daai^6$ fuk^1. Putting the first letters of the three strings together gives us 'wdf'; and because in the Cantonese phonological system, 'd' and 't' are both dental consonants and often conflated in speech, 'd' conveniently slips into 't', hence yielding 'wtf'; and in capitalized form: WTF. What appears to be positive-sounding Chinese characters in fact belies an abbreviated expletive through a combination of transliteration and acronymization. The bottom-left image, which says: Hey Boss, 艾東撈, looks like an instance of code-switching, but in fact it is fully English: 'Hey Boss, I don't know'. Once again, this interpretation is possible only with the knowledge that the three characters, which do not make up a sensible Chinese word, transliterates as $ngaai^6$ $dung^1$ lou^1, a phonetic mimicry of 'I don't know' shot through with a distinctively Hong Kong accent.

The last image on the bottom-right is slightly different. Orthographically it resembles Vietnamese, complete with the diacritics of the Vietnamese script. And even if one can't read Vietnamese, one should suspect this string does not mean anything in that language. One needs to pronounce the words to get at the meaning: *phuc king all some*. Combining the first two words gives us *phucking*, which is homophonous to 'f**king' and a euphemized spelling of the latter expletive; and according to an urban dictionary, it is also a slang word meaning 'machine intercourse'.[48] The last two words combine to give us *allsome* which of course translates into 'awesome'. Hence, underlying the apparently Vietnamese line is the interjection 'f**king awesome'. This example is admit-tedly a marginal one as no Cantonese is involved in its interpretation. Yet it nonetheless bears the G.O.D. brand name and thus can be seen as originating in Hong Kong. Importantly, it demonstrates the deceptive linguistic moves so typical of Kongish in general, where paralinguistic resources such as ortho-graphic elements (the diacritics in Vietnamese writing) are deployed to twist English out of shape – precisely for the reader to put it back into shape.

The question can then be raised as to whether and why the examples in Figure 15d should even be considered Kongish when their linguistic forms are anything but English. But perhaps this is a wrong question to ask, for it assumes that Kongish is some form of English (more on this below). I want to contend

---

[48] https://www.urbandictionary.com/define.php?term=phucking.

that these examples, too, can be included under the Kongish rubric, not just because they embody a translanguaging practice, but also because they are rooted in Hong Kong's street patois, sociocultural artefacts, and collective memory, and constitute the design ethos of text-based commodities rendered marketable by Hong Kong entrepreneurs. Giving them alternative labels like 'Hong Kong Chinese' or 'Cantonese-English' would be equally arbitrary. The issue then arises as to the ontology of Kongish: must Kongish always be 'English' in form? Phrased more radically, the question is this: must Kongish *be* English? How can we question the boundaries between named languages, and indeed the naming of languages per se? We will conclude the present study with these questions in mind.

5 Implications of Study

In light of more recent changes in the city's identity landscape, there is no doubt that the usage of and perception toward English in Hong Kong have experienced shifts of significance to applied linguistics. Thus, Hansen Edwards (2016: 163) suggests that English as it is used in Hong Kong can be said to be inching toward 'endonormative stabilization' in Schneider's (2009) Postcolonial Englishes model or the 'acceptance' pole of localized varieties in Kachru's (1983) World Englishes paradigm. That is to say, HKE is becoming less dependent on exonormative standards benchmarked by British or American English and has become increasingly recognized by local users as an integral component of their parole.

From the perspective of the World/Asian/Postcolonial Englishes paradigm, Hansen Edwards is right. As Hansen Edwards does not differentiate between HKE and Kongish (see Hansen Edwards 2016: 158), her assessment would equally apply to Kongish. Accordingly, the implication is that Kongish must be conceived within the rubric of English(es). There is perhaps an inevitability to this view, owing to the naming of Kongish itself, where the *-ish* ending already affiliates it from the outset with English.

Contrast this view with that put forth by Li Wei, who espouses a non-varietal approach to Kongish and challenges us to consider if Kongish might be conceived not as a *variety* of English, not as any named language as such, but as 'a communicative practice with creative and critical capacity' (Li et al. 2020: 331). According to Li et al. (2020: 311), the editors of Kongish Daily initially introduced their webpage, at the time of its inauguration, as 'a local site sharing news in Hong Kong English (Kongish)'. This latter statement has subsequently been superseded by the claim that *Kongish hai more creative, more flexible, and more functional ge variety* ('Kongish is a more creative, more flexible, and more functional variety'), and one has to assume from the context that 'variety' here refers to 'variety of English'. But in its latest and current statement, Kongish Daily makes a very different proclamation – that *Kongish dou ng exactly hai Hong Kong English* ('Kongish is not exactly Hong Kong English').

These shifts in self-definition on the part of Kongish Daily's editors suggest that Kongish is a dynamic and evolving entity. One might say it is a continuum that stretches from, at the one end, HKE in its prototypical forms to a translingual and multimodal urban dialect, at the other end, one that is much more contingent, creative, and critical. Indeed, there are instances of Kongish communications in Kongish Daily that would still fit within the HKE framework. But to my mind, there is purchase in Li Wei's view of Kongish. As my examples in Section 3 have shown, Kongish exceeds HKE in terms of its linguistic constitution as well as its ethos. Not only is Kongish developing into a translingual practice that has few rules and is concocted by the seat of one's pants; it is also a multimodal register, where numbers and emoji icons are integral to the discourse itself. Finally, it has a self-reflexivity, ludic creativity, and sardonic criticality that is not characteristic of HKE as it is spoken in the streets. This last feature is attested in the commoditization of Kongish, explained in Section 4, which connects with Li Wei's claim that Kongish is a communicative practice, in this case a marketing practice that quite literally puts an urban dialect up *for sale*.

In my view, Kongish is an affective style, a self-conscious metalanguage thriving on its otherness in relation to *either/neither/both* English *or/nor/and* Chinese, and co-opting resources from other languages and non-linguistic repertoires. It may be tempting to correlate its angsty affect and irreverent style to more recent socio-political controversies in Hong Kong, but one needs to be cautious not to make another kind of fetish out of urban dialects by over-investing them with a political valence. Although Kongish came into prominence in the midst of the most testing socio-political times of Hong Kong, its significance should not be reduced to radical identity politics. Rather, Kongish is the effect of the confluence of postcolonial languaging, social media technologies, and civic consciousness, 'captur[ing] sociolinguistic realities of the post-1997 Hong Kong and fill[ing] a gap in Hong Kong media landscape' (Li et al. 2020: 331–2). It is therefore the function of Hong Kong's unique sociolinguistic trajectory, not an abrupt exemplification of particular socio-political events.

On more theoretical grounds, Kongish offers a test case for us to revisit assumptions regarding English in its regional variations. First, it raises questions about the ownership of English: can Kongish users, who are so-called non-native speakers of English – signified by terms like ESL (English as a Second Language), EFL (English as a Foreign Language), and LOTE (Languages Other

Than English) – legitimately and proactively contribute to innovation, and not merely *variation*, in the English language? Assuming for the moment that Kongish is a variety of English, its discursive creativity prompts us to look closely at the 'English or European bias' in perceptions on linguistic variation, that is, the assumption that 'having languages other than English in one's repertoire, even if from birth, somehow dilutes one's competence and raises doubts over one's entitlement to the claim of a native English speaker' (Li 2020: 238). Corollary to this is the 'monolingual bias', manifested as a negative attitude toward language mixing in which '[t]he participating languages are not treated as equal partners: one is the host or matrix language and the other is "the other", guest, or embedded [language]' (Li 2020: 240). On this view, mixing represents an adulteration of the pristine matrix language, always resulting in 'mistakes' and never positive change. Kongish complicates this view, as it is not simply multilingual but immanently heteroglossic. The identities of host/matrix or guest/embedded language are often ambivalent in Kongish, whose surface-segmentable forms cannot be adequately explained by the constructs of codemixing or codeswitching. And lastly, operating on the affordances of Facebook gives Kongish a multimodal edge, enabling it to speak against the 'lingual bias', a perspective that sustains the distinction between the linguistic, the paralinguistic, and the extralinguistic (Li 2020: 241). As my examples in Section 3 illustrate, the extensive use of symbolic resources such as numbers, abbreviations, and emojis in Kongish communications points to a complex semiotics that extends beyond an exclusively linguistic imaginary. And the entextualization of Kongish on merchandise, as explained in Section 4, further speaks to its integration with visual and tactile modalities in text-based objects.

Returning to our earlier question: must Kongish be considered *an* English? At the moment this is a moot point, especially if the very naming of Kong*ish* itself already attaches it indelibly to English by recalling World Englishes – in particular Kong*lish* (note the difference in spelling), which refers to Korean English. I am not suggesting we should change the appellation Kongish; that would risk creating confusion, not to mention that any proposed substitute is likely to be problematic in some other way. But I do want to venture this provocation: that Kongish can potentially lead the way to a reimagining of contemporary urban dialects as a kind of monstrosity, based *off* – with a slightly different implication than based *on* – English but is *not* recognizably English and, better still (thanks to its high intersemioticity), not purely a language as such. At this point it may be apt to remind ourselves of Deleuze and Guattari's (1987 [1980]: 8) understanding that there is no language in itself, nor are there any linguistic universals, only a throng of dialects, patois, slangs, and specialized languages. There is no ideal speaker-listener, any more than there is a homogeneous linguistic community.... There is no mother tongue, only a power takeover by a dominant language within a political multiplicity.

The challenge, then, lies in our capacity to think beyond an X-*ish* appellation (Kongish, Singlish, Frenglish) even while using it; in other words, to think of Kongish as an innominate term beyond named languages. More than that, it is to push the envelope on multilingualism toward post-multilingualism (Li 2018b; Lee 2022a), focusing not on the complementary co-existence of diverse languages, but on the cultivation of a metalinguistic sensitivity among multilingual users to continually experiment with the creative and critical potentialities cutting across linguistic registers and semiotic modalities.

One conceptual route to understanding Kongish in relation to English, I suggest, is via the notion of the Xenophone. Here I want to come full circle by returning to the quote from Rey Chow cited at the opening of Section 1: 'In postcolonial languaging, dispossession is the key that opens unexpected doors. Behind those doors lie the vast, wondrous troves of xenophonic énoncés' (Chow 2014: 60). It is through the dispossession of one's tongue that something else is gained. For Chow (2014: 41), Hong Kong's colonial situation has unwittingly 'conferred upon the colonized the privilege of a certain prescience – the grasp of how artificially and artifactually, rather than naturally, language works and can work in the first place'. If we agree with this statement, then Kongish has come to be part of those 'vast, wondrous troves of xenophonic énoncés', enabling it to circumvent the either/or binaries that constitute the artificial split between English and Chinese, between the written and the spoken, as well as between the verbal and the nonverbal.

What, then, is the implication of Kongish discourse for understanding knowledge production in contemporary Hong Kong? In more recent work, Rey Chow (2021: 125) maintains that '[i]f human language is no longer viewed in the sense of a linear, logical progression but rather as actual discourses found in bits and pieces, human signification would amount to a new type of act – an archiving in process, so to speak, involving shifting series of transitions among different levels of deposits, excavations, adaptations, repurposings, and projections'. To my mind, Kongish discourse embodies such an archiving process, involving 'bits and pieces' of Cantonese and English. As an urban dialect, it registers Hong Kong's linguistic transitioning across its deposits, excavations, adaptations, repurposings, and projections in its continual negotiations between the Anglophone and the Sinophone.

References

África-Vidal, C. 2022. *Translating Borrowed Tongues: The Verbal Quest of Ilan Stavans*. London: Routledge.

Agha, A. 2003. The social life of cultural value. *Language and Communication* 23(3–4): 231–73.

Agha, A. 2007. *Language and Social Relations*. Cambridge: Cambridge University Press.

Agha, A. 2011. Commodity registers. *Journal of Linguistic Anthropology* 21 (1): 22–53.

Anderson, B. 1983. *Imagined Communities: Reflections on the Origin and Spread of Nationalism*. London: Verso.

Appadurai, A. 1986. Commodities and the politics of value. In A. Appadurai (ed.) *The Social Life of Things: Commodities in Cultural Perspective*. Cambridge: Cambridge University Press, 3–63.

Appadurai, A. 1990. Disjuncture and difference in the global economy. *Theory, Culture & Society* 7: 295–310.

Baker, M. 2019. *Translation and Conflict: A Narrative Account* (second ed.). London: Routledge.

Bauman, Z. 2000. *Liquid Modernity*. Boston, MA: Wiley.

Bauman, R. & C. L. Briggs. 1990. Poetics and performance as critical perspectives on language and social life. *Annual Review of Anthropology* 19: 59–88

Becker, A. L. 1995. *Beyond Translation: Essays Toward a Modern Philology*. Ann Arbor, MI: University of Michigan Press.

Blommaert, J. 2008. *Grassroots Literacy: Writing, Identity and Voice in Central Africa*. London: Routledge.

Blommaert, J. & Varis, P. 2015. *Enoughness, Accent and Light Communities: Essays on Contemporary Identities* (Tilburg Papers in Cultural Studies, No. 139), https://research.tilburguniversity.edu/en/publications/enoughness-accent-and-light-communities-essays-on-contemporary-id.

Bolton, K. 2002a. Introduction. In K. Bolton (ed.) *Hong Kong English: Autonomy and Creativity*. Hong Kong: Hong Kong University Press, 1–25.

Bolton, K. 2002b. The sociolinguistics of Hong Kong English. In K. Bolton (ed.) *Hong Kong English: Autonomy and Creativity*. Hong Kong: Hong Kong University Press, 29–55.

Bolton, K. 2011. Language policy and planning in Hong Kong: Colonial and post-colonial perspectives. *Applied Linguistics Review* 2: 51–74.

Bolton, K., Botha, W., & Kirkpatrick, A. (eds.) 2020. *The Handbook of Asian Englishes*. Chichester: Wiley Blackwell.

Bolton, K. & Kwok, H. 1990. The dynamics of the Hong Kong accent: Social identity and sociolinguistic description. *Journal of Asian Pacific Communication* 1: 147–72.

Brown-Saracino, J. 2009. *A Neighborhood That Never Changes: Gentrification, Social Preservation and the Search for Authenticity*. Chicago, IL: University of Chicago Press.

Butler, S. 1997. Corpus of English in Southeast Asia: Implications for a regional dictionary. In M. L. S. Bautista (ed.) *English Is an Asian Language: The Philippine Context*. Manila: The Macquarie Library, 103–24.

Chow, R. 2012. *Entanglements, or Transmedial Thinking about Capture*. Durham, NC: Duke University Press.

Chow, R. 2014. *Not Like a Native Speaker: On Languaging As a Postcolonial Experience*. New York: Columbia University Press.

Chow, R. 2021. *A Face Drawn in Sand: Humanistic Inquiry and Foucault in the Present*. New York: Columbia University Press.

Coupland, N. 2003. Sociolinguistic authenticities. *Journal of Sociolinguistics* 7 (3): 417–31.

Coupland, N. 2007. *Style*. Cambridge: Cambridge University Press.

Coupland, N. 2012. Bilingualism on display: The framing of Welsh and English in Welsh public spaces. *Language in Society* 41: 1–27.

Cowley, S. 2021. Reading: Skilled linguistic action. *Language Sciences* 84 (Article 101364), https://doi.org/10.1016/j.langsci.2021.101364.

Cresswell, T. 2014. *Place: An Introduction* (second ed.). Chichester: Wiley Blackwell.

Crystal, D. 2010. *A Little Book of Language*. New Haven, CT: Yale University Press.

Cummings, P. J. & Wolf, H.-G. (eds.) 2011. *A Dictionary of Hong Kong English: Words from the Fragrant Harbor*. Hong Kong: Hong Kong University Press.

Deleuze, G. & Guattari, F. 1987 [1980]. *A Thousand Plateaus: Capitalism and Schizophrenia*. Trans. B. Massumi. London: Continuum.

Hall, S. 1996. Introduction: Who needs 'identity'? In S. Hall & P. du Gay (eds.) *Questions of Cultural Identity*. London: Sage, 1–12.

Hansen Edwards, J. G. 2015. Hong Kong English: Attitudes, identity, and use. *Asian Englishes* 17(3): 184–208.

Hansen Edwards, J. G. 2016. The politics of language and identity: Attitudes towards Hong Kong English pre and post the Umbrella Movement. *Asian Englishes* 18(2): 157–64.

Heller, M. 2010. The commodification of language. *The Annual Review of Anthropology* 39: 101–14.

Jaworski, A. & Thurlow, C. 2010. *Tourism Discourse: Language and Global Mobility*. London: Palgrave.

Johnstone, B. 2009. Pittsburghese shirts: Commodification and the enregisterment of an urban dialect. *American Speech* 84(2): 157–75.

Johnstone, B. 2010. Indexing the local. In N. Coupland (ed.) *The Handbook of Language and Globalization*. Oxford: Wiley-Blackwell, 386–405.

Johnstone, B., Andrus, J., & Danielson, A. E. 2006. Mobility, indexicality, and the enregisterment of 'Pittsburghese'. *Journal of English Linguistics* 34(2): 77–104.

Jones, Ellen. 2022. *Literature in Motion: Translating Multilingualism Across the Americas*. New York: Columbia University Press.

Kachru, B. B. 1983. Models for non-native Englishes. In K. Bolton & B. B. Kachru (eds.) *World Englishes: Critical Concepts in Linguistics* (Vol. 4). London: Routledge, 108–30.

Kachru, B. B. 1985. Standards, codification, and sociolinguistic realism: The English language in the Outer Circle. In R. Quirk & H. G. Widdowson (eds.) *English in the World: Teaching and Learning the Language and Literatures*. Cambridge: Cambridge University Press, 11–30.

Kachru, B. B. 1992 [1982]. Meaning in deviation. In B. B. Kachru (ed.) *The Other Tongue: English Across Cultures* (second ed.). Urbana, IL: University of Illinois Press, 301–26.

Kellman, S. G. 2020. *Nimble Tongues: Studies in Literary Translingualism*. West Lafayette, IN: Purdue University Press.

Kelly-Holmes, H. 2014. Linguistic fetish: The sociolinguistics of visual multilingualism. In D. Machin (ed.) *Visual Communication* (Vol. 4 of the *Handbook of Communication Science*). Berlin: Mouton de Gruyter, 135–51.

Kelly-Holmes, H. 2020. The linguistic business of marketing. In C. Thurlow (ed.) *The Business of Words: Wordsmiths, Linguists, and Other Language Workers*. London: Routledge, 36–50.

Kirkpatrick, A. (ed.) 2021. *The Routledge Handbook of World Englishes* (second ed.). London: Routledge.

Klein, N. 2000. *No Logo*. London: Flamingo.

Lee, T. K. 2022a. *Choreographies of Multilingualism: Writing and Language Ideology in Singapore*. Oxford: Oxford University Press.

Lee, T. K. 2022b. Moment as method. *Research Methods in Applied Linguistics* 1(3). https://doi.org/10.1016/j.rmal.2022.100015.

Lee, T. K. & Li, W. 2020. Translanguaging and momentarity in social interaction. In A. de Fina & A. Georgakopoulou (eds.) *The Cambridge Handbook of Discourse Studies*. Cambridge: Cambridge University Press, 394–416.

Lee, T. K. & Li, W. 2021. Translanguaging and multilingual creativity with English in the Sinophone world. In A. Kirkpatrick (ed.) *The Routledge Handbook of World Englishes* (second ed.). London: Routledge, 558–75.

Li, W. 1994. *Three Generations, Two Languages, One Family: Language Choice and Language Shift in a Chinese Community in Britain.* Clevedon: Multilingual Matters.

Li, W. 2011. Moment analysis and translanguaging space: Discursive construction of identities by multilingual Chinese youth in Britain. *Journal of Pragmatics* 43: 1222–35.

Li, W. 2016. New Chinglish and the post-multilingualism challenge: Translanguaging ELF in China. *Journal of English As a Lingua Franca* 5 (1): 1–25.

Li, W. 2018a. Translanguaging as a practical theory of language. *Applied Linguistics* 39(1): 9–30.

Li, W. 2018b. Linguistic (super)diversity, post-multilingualism and translanguaging moments. In A. Cresse & A. Blackledge (eds.) *The Routledge Handbook of Language and Superdiversity: An Interdisciplinary Perspective.* London: Routledge, 16–29.

Li, W. 2020. Multilingual English users' linguistic innovation. *World Englishes* 39: 236–48.

Li, W. 2022. Translanguaging as method. *Research Methods in Applied Linguistics* 1(3). https://doi.org/10.1016/j.rmal.2022.100026.

Li, W., Tsang, A., Wong, N., & Lok, P. 2020. Kongish Daily: Researching translanguaging creativity and subversiveness. *International Journal of Multilingualism* 17(3): 309–35.

Love, N. 2017. On languaging and languages. *Language Sciences* 61: 113–47.

Luk, J. C. M. 1998. Hong Kong students' awareness of and reactions to accent differences. *Multilingua* 17: 93–106.

Maher, J. C. 2005. Metroethnicity, language, and the principle of Cool. *International Journal of the Sociology of Language* 175/176: 83–102.

Maher, J. C. 2010. Metroethnicities and metrolanguages. In C. Coupland (ed.), *The Handbook of Language and Globalization.* Chichester: Wiley-Blackwell, 575–91.

Myers-Scotton, C. 1997. *Duelling Languages: Grammatical Structure in Codeswitching.* Oxford: Clarendon Press.

Nelson, G. 2006. *The ICE Hong Kong Corpus: User Manual.* London: University College London.

Ortega y Gasset, J. 1957. What people say: Language. Toward a New Linguistics. In *Man and People*, trans. by W. R. Trask. New York: Norton, 222–57.

Pennycook, A. & Otsuji, E. 2015. *Metrolingualism: Language and the City.* London: Routledge.

Peterson, R. A. & Kern, R. M. 1996. Changing highbrow taste: From snob to omnivore. *American Sociological Review 61*(5): 900–7.

Pietikäinen, S., Jaffe, A., Kelly-Holmes, H., & Coupland, N. 2016. *Sociolinguistics from the Periphery Small Languages in New Circumstances.* Cambridge: Cambridge University Press.

Poon, A. Y. K. 2010. Language use, and language policy and planning in Hong Kong. *Current Issues in Language Planning* 11(1): 1–66.

Raessens, J. 2014. The ludification of culture. In M. Fuchs, S. Fizek, P. Ruffino, and N. Schrape (eds.) *Rethinking Gamification.* Lüneburg, Germany: Meson Press, 91–114.

Rymes, B. 2020. *How We Talk About Language: Exploring Citizen Sociolinguistics.* Cambridge: Cambridge University Press.

Schneider, E. W. 2009. *Postcolonial English: Varieties Around the World.* Cambridge: Cambridge University Press.

Schroeder, J. E. 2006. Editorial: Introduction to the special issue on aesthetics, images and vision. *Marketing Theory* 6(1): 5–11.

Setter, J., Wong, C. S. P., & Chan, B. H. S. 2010. *Hong Kong English.* Edinburgh: Edinburgh University Press.

Sewell, A. & Chan, J. 2016. Hong Kong English, but not as we know it: Kongish and language in late modernity. *International Journal of Applied Linguistics* 27: 596–607.

Shih, S. 2011. The concept of the Sinophone. *PMLA* 126(3): 709–18.

Silverstein, M. 2003. Indexical order and the dialectics of sociolinguistic life. *Language and Communication* 23: 193–229.

Smith, J., & Osborn, M. 2008. Interpretative phenomenological analysis. In J. Smith (ed.) *Qualitative Psychology* (second ed.). London: Sage, 53–80.

Steffensen, S. V. 2015. Distributed language and dialogism: Notes on nonlocality, sensemaking and interactivity. *Language Sciences* 50: 105–19.

Stroud, C. 2015. Linguistic citizenship as utopia. *Multilingual Margins* 2(2): 20–37.

Stroud, C. & Williams, Q. 2017. Multilingualism as utopia: Fashioning non-racial selves. *AILA Review* 30: 167–88.

Theng, A. & Lee, T. K. 2022. The semiotics of multilingual desire in Hong Kong and Singapore's elite foodscape. *Signs and Society* 10(2): 1–29.

Thibault, P. J. 2011. First-order languaging dynamics and second-order language: The distributed language view. *Ecological Psychology* 23(3): 210–45.

Trudgill, P. 1972. Sex, covert prestige and linguistic change in the urban British English of Norwich. *Language in Society* 1(2): 179–95.

Wang, D. D. 2021. Introduction: Chinese literature across the borderlands. *Prism* 18(2): 315–20.

Wee, L. 2018. *The Singlish Controversy*. Cambridge: Cambridge University Press.

Wong, M. 2017. *Hong Kong English: Exploring Lexicogrammar and Discourse from a Corpus-Linguistic Perspective*. London: Palgrave Pivot.

Woolard, K. A. 1998. Simultaneity and bivalency as strategies in bilingualism. *Journal of Linguistic Anthropology* 8(1): 3–29.

Acknowledgements

The author would like to thank Alfred Tsang and Lee Tik Fan for their assistance in the course of this research, as well as the two anonymous reviewers of this manuscript for their valuable suggestions. Special thanks are due to the proprietors of Gweilo, Fok Hing Gin, and Goods of Desire for allowing me to reproduce selected images from their websites. Every effort has been made to contact the copyright owners for the images used in this study, although this may not have been possible in all cases.

The research for this book project is supported by a General Research Fund from the Research Grants Council, Hong Kong SAR (Project number: 17603821).

Cambridge Elements $^{\equiv}$

Applied Linguistics

Li Wei
University College London

Li Wei is Chair of Applied Linguistics at the UCL Institute of Education, University College London (UCL), and Fellow of Academy of Social Sciences, UK. His research covers different aspects of bilingualism and multilingualism. He was the founding editor of the following journals: *International Journal of Bilingualism* (Sage), *Applied Linguistics Review* (De Gruyter), *Language, Culture and Society* (Benjamins), *Chinese Language and Discourse* (Benjamins) and *Global Chinese* (De Gruyter), and is currently Editor of the *International Journal of Bilingual Education and Bilingualism* (Taylor and Francis). His books include the *Blackwell Guide to Research Methods in Bilingualism and Multilingualism* (with Melissa Moyer) and *Translanguaging: Language, Bilingualism and Education* (with Ofelia Garcia) which won the British Association of Applied Linguistics Book Prize.

Zhu Hua
University College London

Zhu Hua is Professor of Language Learning and Intercultural Communication at the UCL Institute of Education, University College London (UCL) and is a Fellow of Academy of Social Sciences, UK. Her research is centred around multilingual and intercultural communication. She has also studied child language development and language learning. She is book series co-editor for *Routledge Studies in Language and Intercultural Communication* and *Cambridge Key Topics in Applied Linguistics*, and Forum and Book Reviews Editor of *Applied Linguistics* (Oxford University Press).

About the Series

Mirroring the *Cambridge Key Topics in Applied Linguistics*, this Elements series focuses on the key topics, concepts and methods in Applied Linguistics today. It revisits core conceptual and methodological issues in different subareas of Applied Linguistics. It also explores new emerging themes and topics. All topics are examined in connection with real-world issues and the broader political, economic and ideological contexts.

Cambridge Elements [≡]

Applied Linguistics

Elements in the series

Viral Discourse
Edited by Rodney H. Jones

Second Language Pragmatics
Wei Ren

Kongish: Translanguaging and the Commodification of an Urban Dialect
Tong King Lee

A full series listing is available at www.cambridge.org/EIAL

Lightning Source UK Ltd.
Milton Keynes UK
UKHW022238240123
415924UK00029B/521